CHRISTIAN MYSTICS

CHRISTIAN MYSTICS

THE SPIRITUAL HEART OF THE CHRISTIAN TRADITION

URSULA KING

SIMON & SCHUSTER EDITIONS

SIMON & SCHUSTER EDITIONS

Rockefeller Center
1230 Avenue of the Americas
New York, NY 10020

A BTB ILLUSTRATED BOOK

Text copyright © 1998 by Ursula King
This edition copyright © 1998 by BTB Illustrated Books
583 Fulham Road, London, SW6 5BY

Printed in China

Library of Congress Cataloging-in-Publication Data
King, Ursula.
    Christian mystics: the spiritual heart of the Christian tradition
    / Ursula King.
      p.   cm.
    Includes bibliographical references and index.
    1. Mystics—Biography. 2. Mysticism—History. 3. Christian saints—biography.   I. Title.
    BV5095.A1K5 1998   97-35806   CIP
    248.2'2'09--dc21
    ISBN 0-684-82423-X

Frontispiece: St. Francis' mystical vision at Mount Alvernia, in which he received
the stigmata. Painting by Giotto (1266-1336). (S. Francesco, Assisi)

Opposite: Jacob's Dream, by William Blake, c. 1805. The religious imagination
has pictured the coming down of God into the world and the human ascent to
the Divine in many different ways. Here, Blake has symbolically expressed it
through the biblical story of Jacob's ladder. (British Museum, London)

$\mathcal{C}$ONTENTS

CHRISTIAN MYSTICS

$\mathscr{I}$NTRODUCTION

A mystic is a person who is deeply aware of the powerful presence of the divine Spirit: someone who seeks, above all, the knowledge and love of God, and who experiences to an extraordinary degree the profoundly personal encounter with the energy of divine life. Mystics often perceive the presence of God throughout the world of nature and in all that is alive, leading to a transfiguration of the ordinary all around them. However, the touch of God is most strongly felt deep within their own hearts.

There are many different kinds of mystic in all religions, and we have in recent years become increasingly aware of their existence and heritage. Many people today are drawn to mystics for inspiration and transformation. They offer a message of wholeness and healing, of harmony, peace, and joy; also of immense struggles fought and won. During the twentieth century we have witnessed destructive events not thought possible in earlier times. We have observed the breakdown of old values, the questioning of traditional ways of life, as well as of the teachings of religion. There is much doubt and searching, and an immense spiritual hunger, especially among the young. To respond to this need and counteract deep existential anguish, many people look to other religious traditions, especially those from the East, to find meaning, direction, and purpose for their lives. Others turn to the sources of their own culture and religion to find answers to their questions, to rediscover the original vision and spirit at the heart of Christianity. For some this is a social gospel or one of liberation, for others it is an inward, mystic call. Yet for many Christian mystics of the past it was a combination of an inner and an outer quest, a journey that led deeply into the divine center of their own souls but then moved outwards again to the concerns of God's created world and those of suffering humanity.

Golden Cell, or Blue Profile, by Odilon Redon, 1893. The word "mystic" is derived from a verb meaning to close one's eyes and lips. This expresses the deep truth that the mystic's consciousness is centered on an inner world of silence and contemplation through which the vision of God is revealed. (British Museum, London)

To rediscover the story of the Christian mystics is a great adventure. Their manifold experiences and examples can be truly empowering for our own lives. Mystics traveled along the margins of the ordinary and the extraordinary, the world of the mundane, and the world of the spirit where all things are made whole. Today, at the beginning of a new millennium, we, too, are finding ourselves at an important threshold of a new, perhaps different and more difficult world, where we can gain much from spiritual nourishment. The Christian mystics speak to us across the centuries and if we listen we can learn something about the deepest experiences of their lives, so that we, too, may glimpse the glory of God and feel the healing touch of the Spirit.

The story of the Christian mystics is one of an all-consuming, passionate love affair between human beings and God. It speaks of deep yearning, of burning desire for the contemplation and presence of the divine beloved. Mystics seek participation in divine life, union, and communion with God. Their desire is kindled by the fire of divine love itself, which moves the mystics in their search and leads them, often on arduous journeys, to discover and proclaim the all-encompassing love of God for humankind.

The unending quest for loving union and communion with God runs like a golden thread throughout the Christian centuries. Mystic experience lies at the very depth of human spiritual consciousness. It is one of great intensity, power, and energy, matched by nothing else. All other relationships count as nothing when compared with the relationship of the soul to God, the intense consciousness of God's love

and presence. Because of this, mystical experience is seen as the heart of all religion, the point of light to which all seekers are drawn.

The vision of God occurs in a dazzling darkness brighter than the brightest light. It is a vision of great splendor and empowerment that mystics ceaselessly describe, even when affirming that it is entirely incommunicable. The long line of Christian mystics represents the great company of such seers who want to pass on to us the precious riches bestowed upon them.

Where can we meet these Christian mystics? How can we catch a glimpse of their experience, a taste of what they found? How can we follow in their footsteps and learn to be lovers of the Divine? We can listen to their stories, trace the lineaments of their inner lives through the words they left behind, and discover in their writings an experience of a God both far and near, as much present in the spark of our soul as in the starry heavens and the universe around us.

In the beginning, Christian mysticism was fed by two streams: the Jewish heritage and Greek thought, especially the contemplative ideal of the latter as taught by the ancient philosophers. At its very core is the experience of Jesus himself as a person filled with divine life who taught his followers about God's love for His creatures and promised them the powerful support of the divine Spirit. The Christian Bible, especially the New Testament, records Jesus' teachings, but also the experiences of his earliest disciples. These texts have been an inspiration for Christian mystics through the ages.

Christian mystics have experienced God in countless ways—as the ultimate Godhead or Ground of Being, as God who is Father but also Mother, or as God intimately present in the humanity of Jesus, in his life, death, and resurrection, or in the glory of the cosmic Christ, or in the presence and gifts of the Spirit. Christian mystics share certain characteristics, but they are all very different individuals who lived in different times and places.

Many mystics are men, but an extraordinary number of the Christian mystics are women. Mystics have been members of religious orders, priests and lay people, ascetics and monastics, and people—married or single—in ordinary walks of life. There are passive mystics—those who reject the world and withdraw from it— and active ones, who are led back into the world and become immersed in a round of activities, profoundly transformed by a new spirit. The great company of Christian mystics truly reflects the iridescent diversity that is humanity. The immense potential of their greatness, as also some of the limits of their vision, resonates in all of us.

Christian mystics have existed ever since the beginning of Christianity and new ones continue to appear. They possess the power to transform themselves and the world around them by following a "way," a teaching about the ascent of the soul to God, about loving union with God expressed through compassionate and selfless love for others that can inspire us to do likewise. Over the centuries, the experience of the mystics has grown into a body of teachings that early Christian writers called "mystical theology." The word "mysticism" is modern, but describes for us what the ancients understood by this "mystical theology:" the communication of an extraordinary experience of great transformative potential for individuals as well as for Church and world.

The story of the Christian mystics vividly communicates the inspiring heritage of a great mystery: the experience of an all-consuming love for both God and the world. It is an experience of a profound spiritual integration that holds the promise of joy and passion, ecstasy, and suffering overcome, a spiritual wholeness and completion that reaches its goal in God. The following pages describe the background and central themes of Christian mysticism, and unfold the story of the most influential mystics of the early Church. The early Christian mystics laid the foundations for the large number of mystics in medieval Europe (Germany, France, Italy, England, and the Low Countries). But the history of Christian mystics did not come to an end with the Reformation; on the contrary, in the early modern period a whole new group of mystics appeared, both in the Catholic Churches of Spain and France and also among several Protestant groups. Yet another rich seam of the Christian mystical tradition is represented by the Eastern Orthodox mystics who lived in the different countries of Eastern Europe. Far from being a tradition of the past alone, the examples of Christian mystics can be found today right across the different Christian Churches around the world. It is the aim of this book to open a window on this rich heritage of Christian mystical experience, which speaks so strongly across time and place to our own need and circumstance. I hope readers will enjoy the new vision they discover through their reading as much as I did through writing this story, and that they will feel strengthened and renewed by it.

CHAPTER ONE

$\mathcal{B}$ACKGROUND AND $\mathcal{T}$HEMES

The formative period of Christian mysticism lies in the first five centuries of our era. Christian experience, doctrine and mystical theology developed then, side by side, based on the life and teaching of Jesus as recorded in the Christian Scriptures. The early Christians understood his message as the revelation of God the Father on earth, in his son Jesus, and of his dwelling within us through the Holy Spirit. They wanted to know and to see God, and sought perfection in following the way of Jesus.

Jesus and his earliest disciples were Jewish, and the fellowship of the early Christians was shaped by their Jewish heritage, not least the world of the Hebrew Bible. But Christian experience moved into a new direction by proclaiming that God had come to earth, taken flesh and lived as a human being in Jesus of Nazareth. As St. John's Gospel says about the Word who was God and was with God: "And the Word was made flesh, and dwelt among us." This affirmation developed into what is called the doctrine of the Incarnation, and it is this, more

than anything else, that marks Christianity and Christian mysticism as distinctive and different from that of other religions.

Christianity is a deeply mystical religion—although some people dispute this because they think of it mostly in institutional terms. At its heart is Jesus's own experience, expressed as "I and the Father are one," the message of utter divine unity. But Jesus also stands for the revelation of the fullness of God's love, poured out over all of humankind in the sending of His Son and of His Spirit. Soon the early Christian theologians formulated the implications of these utterances in the doctrine of the Trinity of one God in three persons—Father, Son and Spirit. Much of Christian mysticism revolves around the experiential realization, embedded in prayer, ritual, ascetic practices and contemplation, of what such a trinitarian and incarnate God was

The Baptism of Christ, by Bicci di Lorenzo (1375-1452). The person of Jesus Christ is the focus of the devotional life of many Christian mystics. The baptism of Jesus, so frequently depicted by Western artists, is an affirmation of the Son by God the Father and the Holy Spirit, and thus represents an important expression of divine unity. (York City Art Gallery, England)

The Burning Bush, School of Raphael, early sixteenth century. The appearance of God to Moses in the Burning Bush is central to both Jewish and Christian mysticism. For mystics this biblical event symbolizes the awe and ardor of the mystical encounter with God. (Vatican Loggia, Rome)

like, of how human beings could know Him and of how they could be at their most intimate with Him.

The Biblical Background

A wealth of scriptural passages have inspired Jewish and Christian mystics alike. Through an allegorical reading of Scripture, the mystical significance of particular texts was heightened so that biblical images and teachings nourished Christian mystics through the ages. In the Hebrew Bible, which Christians call the Old Testament, the book of Genesis includes the idea that the human being is created in the image of God. A fundamental insight for Christian mystical theology, this teaching expresses a vital truth about the relationship between God and his creatures, and also about the nature of the soul. Other important images from the Old Testament

are Jacob's vision of a ladder reaching down from heaven to earth, providing a connection between the two realms; Moses's encounter with God in the Burning Bush on Mount Sinai; Isaiah's awesome Temple vision of the Lord in glory; and the most fertile source of all, the Song of Songs, with its erotic and sexual imagery which was mystically interpreted as symbolizing the relation between the soul and God.

In the Christian scriptures of the New Testament the mystics found important sources in the writings of St. John and St. Paul. St. John's Gospel speaks about God's life in us, and Jesus's call to his disciples to seek holiness and perfection in order to become true "children of God." St. Paul's great mystical experience on the road to Damascus, which changed him from an enemy into an ardent supporter of the early Christians, made him into one of the strongest witnesses to the power of the spirit of Christ "in whom we live, move, and have our being." While the Gospels describe Christ's life, his death and resurrection, the Pauline Epistles bear witness to an intense and deeply transforming faith, rooted both in powerful personal experience and in the community of the early disciples which later became the Christian Church.

Paul describes himself as "a man in Christ," affirming a deep union with the Divine which does not negate his own identity but enables him to live within the divine nature itself: "I live, now not I; but Christ lives within me." He also sings the praises of active love, of charity, inspired by the fire of divine love, and outlines a vision of the cosmic Christ, the Christ who "is all, and is in all."

Many other mystics have had similar experiences. The living encounter with God, as

St. John on the Island of Patmos, by Hans Memling (c. 1430-95). One of the great mystical writers of the New Testament is St. John, author of the fourth Gospel and the Book of Revelation, which he wrote on Patmos. This panel depicts his inspiring vision of the end of the world, culminating in the great circle of the One who is "the first and the last, the living one...alive for evermore." (Rev. 1:18.) (Memling Museum, Bruges, Belgium)

experienced by Paul on his way to Damascus, is so powerful and compelling that the mystic cannot resist the divine summons to a new life. The call to seek God's love above all things becomes a splendid adventure which engages the whole human being, body, mind, and soul. It is an adventure which Christian mystics have pursued by many different paths, but usually in the context of community and fellowship, expressing their love in active concern for others, rather than as a lonely endeavor benefiting only themselves.

The greatest passages on Christian love, on the mutual indwelling of Father, Son, and Spirit, and on the mystery of the Incarnation, are found in St. John's Gospel, where Jesus says at the Last Supper "Love one another as I have loved you." Here the breaking of the bread, the celebration of shared fellowship and communion which is a joyous thanksgiving, or *eucharist*, reveals a profound truth about the interpenetration of spirit and matter, where matter itself becomes a vehicle for the Spirit, a sacrament. The mystics have been nourished by this sacramental spirituality expressed in Jesus's words: "I am that living bread which has come down from heaven: if anyone eats this bread he shall live for ever. Moreover, the bread which I will give is my own flesh; I give it for the life of the world.... Whoever eats my flesh and drinks my blood dwells continually in me and I dwell in him."

Institution of the Eucharist, by Justus of Ghent (1473-4). One of the central rites for Christians is the celebration of the eucharist, or communion, commemorating the last meal of Christ with his disciples. Christian mystics have often experienced mystical union with God through taking the body and blood of Christ during the act of holy communion. (Palazzo Ducale, Urbino, Italy)

The Hellenistic World

Christian mystical theology cannot be understood without its biblical background and the historical and cultural context of the early Church. The early Christians lived within a Hellenistic culture. The development of Christian theology, whether mystical or doctrinal, was deeply influenced by Greek thought patterns. The word "mysticism" is connected with the mystery cults of the ancient Greeks which revealed the knowledge of things divine to an inner circle of initiates, the Gnostics, who alone possessed true knowledge about the nature of reality and the human being. The very notion of the soul is Greek rather than biblical, but it has had a profound impact on Christian experience and thinking. Plato's philosophy, and his description of the soul's journey from appearance to reality, the highest Idea of the Good, the teachings of Neoplatonism, and the mystical philosophy of Plotinus—all influenced Christian thinkers to take up the contemplative ideal, the search for the true knowledge of God.

Mystics are sometimes called the "elect of the elect," or the "friends of God." Mysticism is not unique to Christianity, and the Christian mystics share many characteristics with those of other religions. Yet one must ask to what extent Christian mysticism is the same as or different from mysticism within these other religions.

All mysticism is characterized by a passion for unity. To the mystic, true Being and Ultimate Reality are One. This can be experienced as both impersonal and personal, as Ground of Being, Ultimate Source, Perfect Goodness, Eternal Wisdom, Divine Love, God, or the Godhead.

St. Augustine preaching to his disciples, an illumination from an eleventh-twelfth century edition of *De Civitate Dei*. St. Augustine's works have exercized a lasting influence on Christian theology and mysticism. In his *Confessions* he vividly relates his own encounter with God, whom he describes as "the Life of the life of my soul." (Biblioteca Medicea-Laurenziana, Florence)

This Reality contains, yet transcends, everything there is. It is the One in whom all is lost and all is found.

Christian mystics aspire to an intimate union of love with God, seeking God's presence as the very "ground of the soul." The human being is endowed with a spiritual sense which opens us inwardly, just as our physical senses open us outwardly. Thus St. Augustine of Hippo speaks of the "eye" of the soul and the "ear" of the mind, and others refer to the "eyes of faith" which open us up to higher spiritual realities.

Based on their experiences, mystics have developed a complex set of teachings about divine knowledge and how it is to be obtained. This includes philosophical doctrines about the nature of God, the relation between God and the soul, the soul's journey to God, and the abiding union and intimate love between God and the soul. At a practical level, different rules and exercises have been worked out to help seekers along the path and indicate the stages of the mystic way to communion with God.

Although Christian mystics aspired to true knowledge—a real *gnosis*—of God, they distinguished themselves from the Gnostics and the various forms of Gnosticism in the ancient world, which date back to pre-Christian times. In fact, there was much controversy between Christian and Gnostic writers. The latter were seen as heretics by Christians because of the distinction they made between spirit and matter, God and the world. Their teachings about a distant and absolute Divine Being and an inferior Creator God who had made the material world, including the flesh of human beings, were at variance with the Christian understanding of God and the world. The Gnostics laid claim to esoteric knowledge about God and the universe. They believed in a complex hierarchy of spiritual beings, but communicated this knowledge only to the elect, whereas the Christian message about Jesus was addressed to all. It would have been inconceivable for the Gnostics to accept that God could descend into matter, take up a human body and sanctify the flesh. Martyrdom was a significant aspect of the early Christian Church, before Christianity became an official state religion, and Christian writers defended the reality and dignity of the body, offered up for the love of God and sharing in the sufferings of Christ, which they understood as real.

Asceticism and Monasticism

Early Christian mysticism developed in a context of sharing in Christ's Passion through martyrdom, which was followed by a strong emphasis on asceticism, which in turn led to the development of the monastic life. When Christianity became the official religion of the state in the fourth century, martyrdom was no longer necessary. Those who wished to practice the highest possible perfection opted for an ascetic life, often withdrawing to live in the desert, as Jewish and Egyptian ascetics had done before. The Christian ascetics soon developed the monastic ideal, originally as a solitary life (*monos* meaning "alone" in Greek) pursued by the individual, but monasticism eventually took on a corporate character with rules, teachings handed down from one generation to the next, and leaders.

It was among the early Christian philosophers, ascetics, and monastics that the foundations for Christian mysticism were laid. Many are the personalities who contributed their experiences and teachings, but they stand out much less sharply as individuals than do the Christian mystics of later centuries who often left autobiographical writings. It was the aim of ascetic and monastic life to achieve the conquest of self through renunciation so that, once purified from all obstacles, the soul might live the perfect life face to face with God, in direct communion and union with him. In the silence of the desert, in the solitude of the cell, free from all worldly entanglements, the mystic could ascend to the contemplation and knowledge of God, and loving union with him.

Some people maintain that these early Christians were not really mystics, because their experiences were so different from those of some of the later mystics; or that the mysticism they practiced was not really Christian, but of a Greek philosophical kind, a sort of "philosophical spirituality" which had nothing specifically and originally Christian about it. This can be refuted, however. Although much influenced by its Jewish and Greek background and similar to other forms of mysticism in its passion for the Absolute, Christian mysticism has very distinctive features of its own. While Platonic philosophy stresses the essentially spiritual nature of human beings and their kinship with the Divine, Christianity teaches that they are God's creatures rather than his kin, utterly

Inside the Coptic monastery of St. Antony, about 162 miles south of Cairo, near the Red Sea. Early Christian mystics often found God in the silence of the desert. We can discern traces of their experience in early monasteries and cave dwellings.

St. Catherine's Monastery at Sinai, by Adrien Dauzats (1804-1868). Because of its association with Moses and the Israelites, Mount Sinai, in the desert between Egypt and modern Israel, has been a holy place since ancient times. It became an early center of Christian monasticism. This monastery is much visited today, and contemporary pilgrims may experience something of the mystical attraction and haunting beauty of the desert which can bring us closer to the heart of God. (Private Collection)

dependent on and sustained by him, but created in the image of God which is deeply imprinted in their being. The true nature of the human being is a balanced integration of spirit and flesh, a true unity, not a dualistic separation whereby only the spirit is close to the Divine. Platonic and Neoplatonic writers speak of the soul's ascent to God, whereas Christianity emphasizes the descent of God into the world so that the world and all humanity can become one with God. The mystic's intense longing for such union can be understood in different ways: it can literally mean absorption, fusion, and utter identity, as is the case in many mysticisms, or it can mean the highest consummation of love, where the lover and beloved in their most intimate union still remain aware of each other, as in Christian mysticism.

Love of God

Also very different is the rhythm between contemplation and action which are held together in the ideal of Christian love. For the Christian, the love of God is expressed through the love of Christ, who unites human beings to him, and through him to one another. Thus the experience of the Christian mystic is not the Neoplatonic "flight of the alone to the Alone," but rather occurs in a community context by seeking participation in the mystery of Christ, itself inseparable from the mystery of the Church, the Body of Christ. The Christian mystic is not primarily seen as a privileged individual or a member of an intellectual elite, as among Platonists and Gnostics, but rather as a living cell of the Body of Christ. Thus the mystical life represents the full flowering of Christian baptism

which is the rite of incorporation, the foundational sacrament, for membership of the Church. Because of this, mystical experience is in principle open to all. It is for everybody, not just the elect.

Of great importance also is the concept of God who is not simply One, Ultimate Reality or the Absolute, but a personal Being who yet transcends all notions of personhood found among human beings by forming a community of persons within the mystery of the Trinity. God works mysteriously among human beings through his grace, his inexhaustible love, which creates the very possibility for the soul to seek and love God.

The mystical writer Evelyn Underhill called the mystics the "ambassadors of God." Given the Christian concept of a God of infinite love, however, it would be more appropriate to describe them as "the troubadours of the love of God" who have left us so many of their songs in the form of aphorisms, sayings, poems, hymns, essays, autobiographies—so numerous are the literary genres in which mystical experience has been celebrated and described. We have access today, as never before, to this treasure house of the human spirit. Surveying the rich heritage of Christian mystics, what are some of the main themes that directed and shaped their unending quest for union with God?

The Wheel of Sevens, illumination from the fourteenth-century English Psalter of Robert de Lisle. This great theological and moral diagram was meant to be read both in concentric rings and radial segments. It is like a Christian mandala created by the medieval mind. For the mystic, all things are held in Christ, the God-man, here depicted holding the world at the center of the universe, from which everything radiates. The four evangelists and their symbols frame the circle above the figures of the Virgin and St. Elizabeth, who express a feminine presence and support. (British Library, London)

The ladder of vices and virtues in a sixteenth-century mural from the church at Sucevita in Romania.

Stages on the Path

The way of the mystic has over time been divided into three significant stages through which the mystic had to pass to achieve union with God. It is like a "ladder of perfection," or *scala perfectionis,* which begins with the lowest stage of the *purgative life*, the way of purification, understood as detachment, renunciation, and asceticism, to move away from the world of the senses and the self to the higher, eternally abiding reality of God.

Such purification of the senses and the mind, an utter stripping away which could include many practices of self-mortification, leads to the second stage, which is the *illuminative life*. At this stage the mystic draws nearer to divine unity, reaching the heights of loving contemplation. Fully illumined, he or she realizes the ultimate mystery of all that exists and dwells with joy in a state of sublime ignorance, likened to utter darkness, to an abyss of nothingness.

This is followed by the highest stage, the *unitive life*, the ultimate goal of loving union with God, an ecstatic experience of overwhelming joy. Some mystics have described this experience of union as a spiritual marriage between God and the soul, preceded by a spiritual betrothal during the stage of illumination. Others see the whole mystical journey as a process of "deification"—an important idea in Eastern Orthodox mysticism—but however intimate this union with God is, Christian mysticism never abandons the otherness of God, and the mystic never ceases to be God's creature.

The Ultimate Goal

Christian mysticism can be Christocentric or theocentric, but these forms may also be combined. The mystic's devotion and con- templation can focus on the figure of Jesus Christ, his humanity with its healing ministry, suffering, death, and resurrection, or on Jesus as

Mosaic from the Byzantine church of Hagia Sophia, Istanbul. The majesty and divine spendor of Christ, the Divine Word, found sublime expression in the serene beauty of Byzantine mosaics, whose mystical appeal transcends both space and time. These great artistic creations reflect the harmonious union and deep inner peace experienced by Christian mystics.

the divine Logos and eternal Word, or on the presence of Christ in all things, his divine Lordship as *Pantokrator* or ruler of the universe. There are many passages in the New Testament which inspire such devotions, and numerous Christian mystics give witness to a deeply personal and very intimate experience.

Theocentric mysticism focuses directly on God, on God's Being and attributes. It is here that Christian mystics have been most influenced by the Greek ideal of contemplation and taken over many ideas from Platonic and Neoplatonic philosophy. But Christian mystics also contemplate a triune God—God as Trinity—and God as Creator who inheres with and in his creation. The visible universe reflects the beauty and perfection of the divine mind—expressed in Platonic terms, it is a reflection of its heavenly archetypes—and the image of God is reflected in the human soul.

Whatever mystics try to convey about their knowledge and experience of God, however rapturously and ecstatically they express it, their vision far transcends, in fact explodes, all limits of human description. Given this intrinsic insufficiency of language, Christian mysticism distinguishes its descriptions of God by way of negation or affirmation.

Perhaps most widely used and known is the negative way, the *via negativa* (or apophatic way), whereby anything we say of God is so misleading that it must be denied. God is so unimaginably "other" that we can come to know him only by stripping away, by negating every attribute and description. This is why Dionysius the Areopagite speaks of the "divine darkness" of God, and an unknown medieval mystic refers to the cloud of "unknowing."

The *via negativa* has a great tradition in Christian mysticism both East and West, but it also has its critics. It is a question of whether it is simply a device to cope with the limits of language, or whether it also comprises a certain metaphysics which leads to a rejection of the world, of anything that is not God.

Some Christian mystics have a strong preference for the *via positiva* (or the kataphatic way), which celebrates God in positive terms, affirming the divine perfections whereby God possesses all qualities in a sublime and limitless way. The goodness and beauty of creation, the positive attributes of all created things, the love between human beings can all help to seek, praise, and find God.

The following chapters will show how different mystics have expressed their experience of union with God through the centuries, how particular themes find exemplary expression and embodiment in the life and writings of different individuals. From the early Christian mystics of the first five centuries who laid the foundations for all later Christian mysticism, we shall move on to its flowering in the Middle Ages. After considering the extraordinary richness and diversity of medieval mystics, we shall discuss important mystics of the early modern period, the time after the Reformation, which also produced a number of outstanding Protestant mystics. We shall discover the great mystical tradition of the Eastern Orthodox Church and meet some mystics of the twentieth century.

It is probably true to say that our century shows a greater interest and fascination with the mystics of all ages and faiths than any previous period in history. What can we learn from the great company of Christian mystics? What is the significance of their ceaseless quest today? What use can the human community at the threshold of a new millennium make of the invaluable treasures of Christian mysticism for its own greater good and well-being? Looking at the rich history of the Christian mystics will help us to answer some of these questions.

The Creation of the Sun, Moon and Stars, a stained-glass window from the church of St. Madeleine, Troyes, France. Mystics often use images and symbols drawn from the natural world to describe their innermost experience and vision of God. The radiant light of the sun and of the stars provides a powerful metaphor for the inaccessible light of God's presence.

CHAPTER TWO

EARLY CHRISTIAN MYSTICS

How did Christian mysticism begin? There is no one person, no definite date, no single occurrence that represents the clear starting point of the Christian mystical quest; but the main reason and prime inspiration for seeking God above all was Christ's own example, and his command, "Be perfect, as your heavenly Father is perfect" (Matt. 5:48).

Christian life and faith were based on the desire to seek and find God by following Jesus's teachings and his "way," as described in the Gospels. How this should be done was, however, understood quite differently by different people, and soon a mystical theology developed which drew its inspiration from diverse sources. The burning desire for union with God is vividly documented in the lives of the early Christian martyrs and saints, but for a more explicit reflection on the nature and goal of Christian life we need to turn to early Christian theologians and writers. What we know about their encounter with God is based on the documents they left us. By reading them we can discern not

only their personalities and voices, but also some of the dynamics of their social and political worlds, so different from that of our own.

The story of the emergence of Christianity as a new religion in the Roman Empire is fascinating and complex. The context and growth of Christian life was not at all like what we in the West now think of as Christianity. Its institutions and thought patterns developed in countries around the Mediterranean long before the coming of Islam, among peoples formed by the classical worlds of Greece and Rome, in ancient Palestine, Egypt, North Africa, Syria, and Arabia. It was a time of Roman power politics and colonialism, a time of uncertainty and persecution, when the mystery cults and teachings of Oriental religions gained

St. Jerome in his Study, by Antonello da Messina (1430-79). One of the most influential early Christian writers, St. Jerome was the first to translate the Bible into Latin. He traveled widely over the Christian world, living for some years as a hermit in the Syrian desert before returning to Rome and finally settling in Bethlehem. The place of his writing would have been much simpler than that depicted in this painting. (National Gallery, London)

The dedicated fervor and peaceful concentration of early Christian prayer has been immortalized in this fresco in the catacomb of St. Priscilla in Rome. The first Christians prayed standing with arms raised, in an attitude known as orant.

ascendancy throughout the Roman Empire. There was a hunger for new certainties and new knowledge (*gnosis*), and the teachers who offered instruction and promised enlightenment were many.

It was during the second century that a common Christian belief system, a *regula fidei*, was formulated, and the most important institutions and practices of the Church came into existence. It is also during this time that we find the earliest Christian writers on mystical theology in North Africa and the Middle. East. Many of their arguments deal with the nature of "saving knowledge" (*gnosis*) or acquaintance with God brought by Christ. Gnosticism may have arisen independently from Christianity among Jewish sectarians, yet many, perhaps even most, Gnostics of that time thought of themselves as Christians. A proliferation of different Gnostic groups and sects came into existence in early Christianity. They all shared a profoundly dualistic view of reality which posed a threat to the early Church. The material world was rejected as false and evil, whereas salvation was found through true *gnosis*, or knowledge about the innate divinity of the soul and its eventual return to the Highest One, the ultimately Unknowable Source of all spiritual beings.

The beginnings of Christian mysticism occurred during the second century in North Africa, then a thriving center of Roman culture. Carthage and Alexandria were second in importance in the world only to Rome. Alexandria was the center of commerce between Europe and the East, but was also a focal point of Greek and Semitic learning. Here the Hebrew Scriptures were translated into Greek (*Septuagint*), and the Jewish thinker Philo produced a synthesis between Greek philosophy and Jewish theology. Greek scholarship and science reached some of their highest development in Alexandria. Founded by Alexander the Great in 334 B.C., the city had at first been a center of Greek culture in Egypt, then the leading provincial capital of the Roman Empire. Its library and museum were famous throughout the ancient world. Soon the city was attracting members of the new Jesus movement who searched for learning and desired to combine their faith with the insights of Greek philosophy.

According to tradition, St. Mark made his first Christian convert in Alexandria as early as the year 45, and thus opened a new phase in the history of the city. We know little about these early years, but during the second century an important Catechetical School was founded in Alexandria to propagate Christianity among the educated classes. Christianity originally spread in cities rather than in the countryside, and the rise of early Christian mysticism is also connected with the city. It developed from the city to the desert, rather than the other way round.

During the second and third centuries, outstanding members of the Christian community at Alexandria—Clement and Origen—developed a synthesis between the true knowledge of God and the Christian faith. They asserted that God, the Unknown, can be apprehended by following the threefold path of purification, illumination, and union achieved through loving contemplation.

The development of Christian mysticism was subsequently much shaped by the experiences of ascetics and monastics who, under the influence of Clement and Origen, withdrew to the desert where they devoted themselves to the contemplation of God and to extreme ascetic practices, already known to Jews and Egyptians. Their rigorous *askesis* (exercizes) marked them out as "athletes of the spirit." The other-worldliness of their discipline, which has been compared to Yogic and Zen practices, often meant a rejection of earthly life and a contempt for the world and the body.

Virginity became the highest ideal. It profoundly influenced the lives of the monastics who first lived alone in a cell or hut, or as hermits and anchorites in the desert, then formed themselves into communities under the rule of a common superior. This established the pattern for Western monasticism, through which the individual soul could find perfection, ascend to the highest ideals of the spiritual life, and achieve mystical union with God, but also be of service to other human beings through prayer and active good works.

Such ascetics and monastics, both men and women, were found in great numbers in Egypt, North Africa, Syria, Arabia, and Palestine. Their ascetic practices and mystical teachings laid the foundations for all future mystics of Western and Eastern Christianity, and in later centuries they would influence the early mystics of Islam.

It is a matter of some debate as to who might be counted as the first known Christian mystic, since the early personalities and voices are often less distinct than those of more recent times. Their individuality is less easy to discern, and few personal details are known. The major Christian writers of the second half of the second century—Justin, Irenaeus and Clement—all wrote against the Gnostics, but still used some Gnostic ideas in arguing for the truth of the

Christian faith. Clement of Alexandria, in particular, is considered the first writer on mystical theology, and his views influenced many later mystics.

Clement of Alexandria (c. 150-c. 215)

Clement was born and brought up in Athens. As a young man he traveled and studied in different places of learning in Italy and the eastern Mediterranean area, but was particularly drawn to Alexandria, the intellectual center of his time. There he became a pupil of Pantaenus, the first leader of the Christian Catechetical School, founded for the teaching of the Christian faith to those of culture and education. Much influenced by Greek philosophy, the school was Platonist in orientation.

Through Pantaenus' teaching, Clement was converted to Christianity and eventually himself became a teacher at the Catechetical School. In 190 he succeeded his mentor as leader of the school. He held this position until 202, when he fled from Alexandria during the persecution of Christians by the Roman emperor Septimius Severus. Clement found refuge and employment with a former student, Alexander, bishop of Jerusalem, with whom he stayed until his death sometime between 211 and 215.

During his time in Alexandria, Clement was one of the major intellectual leaders of the Christian community there. He wrote several theological works and biblical commentaries, not all of which have survived. Some of the students he taught later became theological and ecclesiastical leaders in the Church; among them was Origen, who followed him.

Although thoroughly loyal to the Church, Clement was deeply influenced by Greek philosophy. Plotinus was his near contemporary, and Platonic and Neoplatonic ideas are found throughout his writings. He drew on them for his interpretation of the Christian faith. While some of his contemporaries denied the importance of philosophy for the life of faith, Clement considered philosophy to be another divine gift to humanity, in addition to the gift of Christ, the Logos, or Word. Clement was one of the early thinkers of the Church who wrestled with the relationship of Christian faith to philosophy and culture. The beginnings of true Christian Platonism and humanism are found in his thought.

Clement was kept busy with several theological and other disputes concerning social justice and Christian witnessing. His polemics were addressed to two different audiences. First there were the Gnostics, who argued that salvation could be reached only through esoteric knowledge or illumination, but not through faith. Against them Clement upheld faith as the basis of the whole spiritual life, but he agreed that "true gnosis" was also an important element in the Christian faith, necessary for acquiring true spiritual and mystical knowledge. Faith must precede understanding. But its ultimate aim is the assimilation to God so that a person may become righteous, holy, and endowed with wisdom. Then there were those Christians who were content with faith alone but did not seek deeper understanding. In fact, they

Clement of Alexandria, shown in an illumination from a twelfth-century Greek manuscript. For Clement the chief teacher is the risen Christ, who spoke through the Hebrew prophets and who continues to teach us through the Holy Spirit. (Bibliothèque National, Paris)

denied the value of philosophizing. But Clement argued against them, saying that there is an integral connection between faith and knowledge or "true gnosis."

Clement's major and best-known works are the *Paedagogos* ("The Teacher") and *Stromateis* ("Miscellanies"). It is in them that we find his ideas on the nature of "true gnosis," the vision of and union with God, and the divinization of the human being. He was a rather unsystematic writer, yet he introduced some of the key ideas which became central to Christian mysticism. Later commentators on his works have sometimes speculated on whether Clement himself ever enjoyed mystical experiences; but this is one of those questions which must remain forever unanswered.

It may be going too far to call Clement the founder of Christian mysticism, but he was certainly an innovator in combining his faith with Platonic philosophy. He appropriated certain mystical themes from Plato, although he was fully aware of the difference of his own views, which were firmly grounded in the Christian Scriptures. He was the first writer to introduce the words "mystical" and "mystically" into Christian literature.

There is no doubt about the depth of Clement's dedication to the incarnate Christ, who is the true teacher of all. He did not consider true gnosis a precondition for salvation, or teach that gnosis is something innate, that the soul has a divine core. Yet the idea that one who has true gnosis is superior to the simple believer is central to his thought. For him it is the gift of Christ—but a gift that can also be acquired and perfected through training. The goal and fruit of true gnosis is the vision of God, the full vision of the pure in heart enjoyed in heaven, but its attainment begins on earth in this life as a gradual process linked to the practice of virtues and moral perfection. It also includes the cultivation of detachment and "passionlessness" or perhaps serenity, and leads to the gift of deification.

Clement was the first to speak extensively of human "divinization," or "becoming like God," as a goal of Christian perfection. Supported by biblical texts, he held the view that God divinizes the human being through his teaching in Christ. His view is summed up in his famous sentence, "I say the Logos of God became man so that you may learn from man how man may become God." The theme of Christian divinization was further developed by the Greek Church Fathers and retains great importance in Orthodox Christianity. Inspired by both Platonic ideas and biblical texts, they could see a congruence between the believer's identification with Christ, the God-man, and the teaching of Greek philosophers about the goal of human existence. From the Jewish thinker Philo, Clement borrowed the idea that God is to be sought, as Moses sought Him, in darkness, and reached by faith, reasoning, and knowledge. But the grace of knowing comes from God through His Son. Clement speaks of three stages of the search, likened to the three days of Abraham's journey. The first stage is the perception of beauties, the second is the desire of the good soul, and in the third the mind sees spiritual things, "the eyes of the understanding being opened by the Teacher who rose again the third day." The highest contemplation is a special gift. It is then that the divine image is sealed upon the soul, which was made in God's image, by the Son, who is the perfect Image.

Clement emphasized the ultimate un-knowability and inexpressibility of God in order to highlight Christ as the only path we have into the Divine Abyss. He used familiar Platonic ideas for expressing this apophatic approach to the

Omne bonum, "All is well," a fourteenth-century encyclopedia of universal knowledge. In this illumination, God's radiance reaches into every corner of the universe. In the middle panel, the light of His countenance is glimpsed by mystics such as St. Benedict and St. Paul. In the bottom panel, Adam and Eve, at the moment of the Fall, are cut off from the divine light. (British Library, London)

divine mystery, thereby showing that philosophical thoughts perfectly agreed with St. John's words that "no one has ever seen God; it is only the Son, who is nearest to the Father's heart, who has made him known" (John 1:18).

Clement was also the first to emphasize the twofold goal of contemplation and action, a theme much developed by later mystics. In the story of Mary and Martha in St. Luke's Gospel (10:38-42), Martha is presented as a symbol of the active life and Mary as that of the contemplative life. These are later often seen as two basic stages of the spiritual journey, although the emphasis on their significance varies greatly. The assessments of Clement's contribution to Christian mysticism vary widely, depending on the acceptability of his use of Greek ideas in the formulation of his thought. But there can be no doubt that this Alexandrian theologian laid much of the groundwork for later Christian mystical theology by the introduction of some of its key ideas. These deeply influenced many other Christian mystics, not least his successor, Origen.

Origen (c. 185-c. 254)

Origen, called "the Adamant" by his contemporaries, is one of the most influential and controversial theologians of the early Church. Sometimes described as "master mystic," he exercised a tremendous influence on Christian spirituality and mystical piety. His mysticism is deeply nourished by biblical thought, and much of his life's work was concerned with drawing out the allegorical and spiritual meanings of scriptural texts. Origen spoke of rising above senses and shadows to one mystical and unspeakable vision. Surrounded by loyal disciples, he lived a life of asceticism, abstinence, and strict discipline to find this ultimate vision of God.

Who was this towering, influential figure, so often quoted by later writers? Born in Alexandria of Christian parents, Origen was educated in the same milieu that produced Clement of Alexandria and Plotinus, and was the first Church teacher to come from a Christian background. His father died in 202, during the persecution of Septimius Severus from which Clement had fled. Origen was attracted to seek the glory of martyrdom for himself and thereby prove the strength of his faith, but his mother prevented him from doing so. Instead, he had to provide for her and his six younger brothers, earning money by teaching while following a life of strict asceticism. It is said that as a young man he took the biblical words "...there are eunuchs who have made themselves eunuchs for the sake of the kingdom of heaven" (Matt. 19:12) literally and castrated himself in order to ensure a life of complete chastity. Later in life, however, he deplored such rigorous fanaticism.

Origen studied under Clement and after the latter's flight from Alexandria succeeded him as head of the Catechetical School. He became thoroughly familiar with Greek philosophy, especially Neoplatonism, but also learned Hebrew and became a great authority in biblical scholarship. He was so much drawn to study and research that he employed a junior colleague to do most of his teaching at the school, thus

Christ in the house of Mary and Martha, an illumination from the Queen Mary's Psalter, early fourteenth century. Christ's conversation with Mary and Martha was read by Christian mystics as an exemplary story of the inner and outer aspects of the spiritual life. (British Library, London)

leaving him free for studying, writing, and traveling. Soon Origen was busy producing many exegetical, doctrinal, and devotional writings as well as polemical works. Much sought after as a preacher, he led a very active life, traveling to Rome, Greece, Arabia, Antioch, and Palestine, and becoming involved in ecclesiastical disputes. He had some notable students who praised his worth and great talents, whereas his enemies found much to criticize. He was a very controversial figure, both in his lifetime and afterwards, but was recognized as a great teacher whose main achievements were his work on the Greek text of the Old Testament and his commentaries on the whole Bible. His orthodoxy was later much debated, Christian writers in the West generally judging him more favorably than those in the East.

Origen was the most important Christian thinker before St. Augustine. He wrote in Greek and stressed the spiritual meaning of biblical texts. His *Commentary on the Song of Songs* is a mystical interpretation, representing union of the soul with God.

In 215, when Alexandrian Christians were massacred in what came to be known as "The Fury of Caracalla," Origen was forced to leave the city. He went to live in Caesarea Maritima, in Palestine, where he opened another school which attracted many students. This was now the base for his activities until the year 250, when he was imprisoned and tortured during the persecution of the emperor Decius. He survived this ordeal, but died soon afterwards, in about 254, in Tyre, where his tomb was long held in honor and still known during the period of the Crusades.

One of the greatest exponents of the allegorical interpretation of Scripture, Origen searched the Bible for the "secret and hidden things of God." Beyond the literal meanings of the texts there exist spiritual meanings, which have to be discovered for God's ways and message to humankind to be understood. Fundamental to Origen's mystical theology is the idea that the soul's beauty consists in being created in the image of God so that there exists a kinship between the human mind and God. There is a progressive revelation of God in the Bible and a progressive growth of the spiritual life in the believer.

For Origen, Christianity provides a ladder of ascent to the Divine, and the Church can be seen as a "great school of souls." After baptism the Christian passes through purgation and illumination, gradually progressing to a final knowledge of God, a God whose essential nature is goodness and who seeks the love of his creatures, but desires a love that is freely given. The transcendent God is the source of all existence who, through his overflowing love, created all things and thereby accepted a degree of self-limitation. God created rational and spiritual beings through the Logos, which became incarnate, living and dwelling in Jesus Christ, whose role is essential in bringing the believer to God. But Jesus appears differently to different people, according to their spiritual capacity. While some see nothing extraordinary in him, others recognize him as their Lord and God, the union of God and man. In his commentary on St. John, Origen dwelled on the titles of Christ, such as Lamb, Redeemer, Wisdom, Truth, Light, and Life. Christ, the Son, who leads to the One who is the Father, has many different aspects, which are like rungs on a ladder of mystical ascent to the beatific vision of God.

For Origen, the mystery of union between the soul and God, as well as that of the Church and God, is symbolically most beautifully expressed in the Song of Songs, of which he was the first Christian interpreter. His commentary on this text from the Hebrew Bible has been preserved only in part, and then only in its Latin translation, but it is based on the claim, already held by the Jews, that the meaning of this ecstatic love poem is really a spiritual one.

Origen's interpretation yields three different levels of meaning. On the first level the Song of Songs is simply a wedding poem, an expression of passionate, intimate love between a rustic bride and a royal bridegroom. On the second level it represents Christ's love for his Church. On the third, mystical level it expresses the deep yearning of the soul to be made one with the divine Word. The Song of Songs thus ultimately becomes the story of the union of the soul with God.

Origen also took up the theme of Martha and Mary, of the active and contemplative life. This distinction, together with many other ideas about the spiritual life and the nature of Christian perfection, was passed on to those who followed him. His world-denying attitude and temperament were a strong influence on the Greek ascetic tradition and the Latin West. His example and teachings soon helped to shape the beginnings of Christian monasticism. It was among the early Christian ascetics and monastics that Christian mysticism found its definite expression, creating a specific pattern, vocabulary, and orientation which was to shape Christian ideals for many centuries.

Ascetics and Monastics (third to fifth centuries)

Christians of the early Church soon developed a desert spirituality based on the thought of Clement and Origen, who saw the vision of God as the goal and end of human life. Both had emphasized the combination of asceticism and mysticism which eventually became the basis for Christian monasticism. Inspired by the example of Christ himself, led by the Spirit into the wilderness and tempted there by the devil, many Christian disciples withdrew into the solitude of the desert to seek Christian perfection through a life of ascetic denial and withdrawal from the world. They were passionately searching for God, yet now no longer in the cities and centers of learning, but in the desert where they devoted themselves to a life of renunciation and celibacy.

Ascetic ideas developed early in the Christian community with its preaching of the imminent coming of the kingdom of God. The early Christians expected the end of the world soon

The Martyrdom of St. Lawrence at the Hands of Decius, by Fra Angelico (c. 1387-1455). Many early Christians experienced martyrdom. Like St. Lawrence, Origen suffered violent persecution by the Roman emperor Decius. The courageous witness of the martyrs provided a lasting inspiration for other Christian saints and mystics for centuries to come. (Chapel of Nicholas V, Vatican)

and awaited Christ's return, his "Second Coming," in prayer, hope, and faith. This led to a sense of detachment from the surrounding world and its concerns. Soon the demand for *askesis*, or discipline, already advocated in the New Testament, led to the counsel of seeking continence, abstinence, and physical hardships of all kinds in order to attain a higher spiritual goal. A certain depreciation of the body, of sexual relations, and marriage developed which may well have been due to Eastern and Gnostic influences. Groups of virgins and ascetics were already present in second-century Christian congregations, and Origen and his group of disciples in Alexandria are a good example.

These early ascetics were not in any way organized; they did not live in communities apart or wear special dress. They worked for the good of the Church and the poor, and were part of their local congregation. Yet they followed certain ascetic practices, kept particular hours of prayer, and also worshipped apart from the congregation as a whole. As social customs of the time exacted a greater standard of modesty and withdrawal on women, who in any case were not allowed to perform pastoral duties as freely as men, devout Christian women formed groups of virgins dedicated to God even before groups of male ascetics had become an accepted norm.

Gradually these ascetics withdrew from their congregations in the city into more rural surroundings and greater isolation. They then moved from inhabited places to tombs and abandoned settlements, into mountains and caves, and eventually into complete isolation in the wilderness of the Egyptian desert. This progressive withdrawal from city life was also much influenced by the repeated persecution of Christians by different Roman emperors. Particularly severe was Trajanus Decius, who was the first to persecute Christians throughout the entire empire. Whereas before him persecutions had been sporadic and local, he issued an edict in the year 250 ordering all citizens to make sacrifices to the state gods in the presence of Roman officials. The penalty for disobedience was death, and countless Christians who defied the government lost their lives, including the bishops of Rome, Jerusalem, and Antioch. It was during this persecution that Origen suffered torture.

Thousands of others fled to exile in the mountains and deserts. Solitude was thus forced upon them rather than chosen. There were individual ascetics, however, who stood out through their absolute dedication to a solitary life of renunciation. They were also much inspired by the example of Christian martyrs who had given up their life for God. Since Christ himself had died on the cross, obedience to death was part of the Christian calling, and death through martyrdom was the supreme trial of faith.

Early in 251, Decius had to abandon his persecution. Public opinion condemned the extreme violence of the government and applauded the passive resistance of Christians whose movement became strengthened rather than weakened through persecution and martyrdom. By 313, when the emperor Constantine promised all Christians state protection in his edict of Milan, the Church became more established, and martyrdom ceased to be an option. It was easier for Christians to live in the world, and their conduct became more lax. The only alternative for

Vision of the Lamb, an illumination from the eighth-century *Commentary on the Apocalypse* by the Spanish monk Beatus de Liebana. This shows the mystical circle of the lamb surrounded by four winged creatures, interpreted as the four evangelists, who sing by day and night the praise of the Holy One (Rev. 4). (Pierpont Morgan Library, New York)

sincere Christian dedication was now a life of rigorous asceticism, where the "athletes of the spirit" could fight against the world, the flesh, and the devil.

The desert, with its vast and lonely spaces, was considered an abode of demons, a place of refuge for the ancient pagan gods. Struggling against these demons and their own inner temptations, exercizing physical restraint, and suffering hardships of all kinds, the ascetics trained their bodies and minds, conquered sin, practiced virtues and unceasing concentration in prayer in view of one great end: to achieve the contemplation of God in purity of heart. The loneliness of the desert was where God was found; it was also the place where temptation was strongest, because it came from the depths within, not from distractions without. This was

The Qumran caves, where the Dead Sea Scrolls were discovered. The early Christians were not the first to seek refuge in the desert. Jewish groups such as the Essenes and others preceded them, and created communities dedicated to the ascetic and spiritual life.

the place *par excellence* where the soul could find union with God, or, as later mystics so vividly described it, a union of iron and fire.

These ascetics may seem to us rather distant and irrelevant. Some undertook extraordinary contortions and excesses, whether standing on a pillar for years, having an arm permanently raised in the air, or going to excessive lengths in fasting, which seem strange and inhuman to us. Yet in spite of all aberrations, the lives of these desert saints, both men and women, who under the stress of persecution fled from the inhabited world and devoted themselves to meditation and prayer in great solitude, contain a great deal of courage and wisdom, and contributed much to the growth of Christian mysticism. Mystical life might also occasionally have developed spontaneously, as it did in the early Church with the Christ-mysticism of St. Paul and St. John, but it generally needed a specific discipline, a conscious preparation and practice, which evolved gradually in the Church. At the level of thought, this development was fostered by the contact of Christianity and Platonism; at the level of practice, it was much shaped by the desert experience of ascetics and monastics.

Of course, asceticism started well before Christianity. We know of Jewish asceticism among the ancient Hebrew prophets, and among the Qumran community near the Dead Sea. John the Baptist had lived an ascetic life in the wilderness, and there was pagan asceticism too. It is known that a community of ascetics lived in the Egyptian desert as early as 340 B.C., and it was in Egypt that Christian asceticism first flourished, from which early Christian monasticism developed. From Egypt, ascetic and monastic forms of life spread to the rest of North Africa,

The Penitence of St. Jerome, by Nicoli di Pietro (1394-1430). The desert was a place not only for encountering God but also for overcoming the temptations of the world and the flesh. Such temptations were vividly experienced in solitude as one's own inner lusts and imperfections. (Louvre, Paris)

to Syria, Palestine, Mesopotamia, and Persia—the whole of the ancient Near East.

At first the ascetics lived alone, as hermits and anchorites who developed the monastic ideal as a solitary life of perfection and renunciation. After the persecutions were over, and Christianity became the official religion of the Roman Empire, devout Christians refused to compromise with the world in the way the Church had now consented to do. They wanted to maintain the old standards of purity and renunciation. Their main way of expressing their absolute dedication and fervor consisted in living apart from the world and following a life of poverty, practicing obedience to a spiritual leader, chastity, and various forms of bodily austerities.

From the beginning, men and women alike followed the ascetic and monastic life, and words of practical wisdom exist from desert fathers and mothers. Perhaps the best known work of this kind, which did much to disseminate the ideal of the ascetic life and solitary monasticism in the western world, is *The Life of St. Antony*. Written by St. Athanasius, it describes the life and temptations of the hermit Antony, who is said to have lived for over a hundred years, from about 251 to about 356, in the Egyptian desert. This hermit ideal captured the

Byzantine manuscript illumination showing Christian martyrs. Martyrdom, whether by fire, decapitation, or other means, was an experience of great spiritual significance for early Christians—one that touched the lives of many saints and mystics. (Biblioteca Nazionale, Turin, Italy)

Christian imagination. Antony's struggle with the demons of the desert was seen as a model of Christian life and was often depicted in Christian religious art in the West.

The solitary life offered much opportunity for ceaseless, undistracted contemplation; it also demanded great endurance and provided many occasions for mortification. But in practice such complete renunciation also meant utter loneliness, which could easily lead to eccentricity and even madness. Self-denial could develop into an exaltation of suffering and *askesis* become an end in itself rather than a means to find God.

Thus new theories developed about the best way of finding God and leading the ideal Christian life. Soon it was thought better to practice renunciation in a group, under the guidance of a wise leader, and not to become a hermit until one had first spent many years in a community. By about the fourth century, groups of monks, each living originally in a single cell or hut, came together to live under the same roof and follow the rule of a common superior. In this way the monastery as we know it developed. The monk withdrew from the world out of love of God and neighbor; the monastic life was intended to bring perfection to the individual soul, which was then

The Decapitation of St. Fabian, from the circle of Jaume Huguet, fifteenth century. St. Fabian was Bishop of Rome and one of the first to suffer martyrdom under the Emperor Decius in 250. He was buried in the catacombs in Rome. (Musée Bonnat, Bayonne, France)

to be used in the service of others, whether by prayer or good works.

Contemporary with St. Antony was Pachomius (about 290-346) who wrote the first rule for monks to regulate their communal life. This rule governed the development of cenobitic, or communal, monasticism, which eventually replaced the eremitic, or solitary type of ascetic life. It was the generally accepted monastic rule until the sixth century, when St. Benedict of Nursia, in central Italy, wrote the Benedictine rule, which gave medieval monasticism its definite and lasting shape in the West.

Pachomius is said to have founded nine monasteries for men, containing some three thousand monks, and two for women. In many parts of the Roman Empire women lived as ascetics, deaconesses, prophetesses, and nuns. Women recluses had been known in earlier, pagan times. Women held a high position in the early Church and were drawn to celibate life before men. Unencumbered by marriage, they were free to devote themselves totally to the

Illumination from a Commentary on the monastic rule of St. Benedict. Several monastic rules provided important foundations for Christian ascetics and monks, but it was St. Benedict's rule that would eventually give shape to Western monasticism. (Abbey of Monte Cassino, Italy)

St. John the Baptist in Meditation, by Hieronymus Bosch (c. 1450-1516). Contemplative meditation is solitary and can take place in different settings—in the desert, in an exotic wilderness, as in this picture, or in a modern urban context. Contemplative and mystical experiences often occur when in contact with nature. (Museo Lázaro Galdiano, Madrid)

ideals of Christian life and perfection, seeking God with all their heart. The strength of Christianity lay in many ways in its female members, who were prominent among the martyrs and contributed much to the growth of Christianity.

Clement of Alexandria had taught that women and men shared a common grace and salvation, and that their virtue and training was alike. In his time women studied the Scriptures, followed the instructions of Christian teachers—Origen had a number of women pupils—and participated fully in the development of asceticism and monasticism in Egypt. They lived as recluses in the desert and followed a life of asceticism as strenuous as that of men. It seems that ascetic communities came earlier into existence among women than men. In fact, such female religious communities existed in Egypt as early as the middle of the third century.

A century later thousands of women were known to live in convents, and one city near Cairo is said to have held as many as twenty thousand nuns. A common pattern seems to have been that of double monasteries for men and women. The convent was at some distance from the monastery, usually divided by the river Nile; the men worked at agriculture and handicrafts to support the women with their surplus, and the women made clothes for the men. An abbess was

Rock-cut church in Cappadocia, Turkey, showing a mural where the tufa has fallen away. The remains of cave monasteries and churches in different parts of the Middle East are a lasting reminder of the thriving communities of early Christian seekers.

in charge of the women just as the men were led by their abbot. Some of the life of these monks and nuns is described in *Paradise of the Fathers,* an account of Egyptian monasticism compiled at the request of a court official in the early fifth century. Christian women following the ascetic life were also found elsewhere in North Africa, Palestine, Syria, and in other parts of Asia Minor.

Drawn mainly from the well-to-do, but also from courtesans and dancers, the holy women were described as "manly" in their courageous attempts to seek perfection, the vision of God, and give service to the poor and needy. There are many women known by name—Mary of Egypt, Pelagia, Melania, Sylvania, Candida, Paula, Macrina, and many others. Some have been dubbed "harlots of the desert" since they had pursued the monks to tempt them, but overcome by the men's holiness, they renounced their own way of life, and withdrew into convents or solitude to seek repentance, divine forgiveness, and the greater beauty of God. Their stories were told by the ancient monks, then translated into Latin and various vernacular languages. They circulated freely in the medieval world of Western Christianity, illustrating both the power of sexual desire and the insight that such desire can also lead to God. The stories of the "harlots" express both the bondage of desire and the fire of love into which human longing is transformed, once an all-consuming love of the Divine becomes its sole object.

In early Christianity a great number of both women and men were prepared to renounce the world and live an ascetic, monastic life. They were honored and revered for their sanctity, both during their life and at shrines after their death, for they provided a high example of Christian life for others to emulate. Soon the cult of male and female saints developed, crowned by that of the Virgin Mary, who was given the title "Mother of God" (*theotokos*) in 431. Venerated throughout the Christian world, a woman was now mediator between God and human beings. This laid the foundation for the development of a rich Marian doctrine which influenced Christian mysticism in the high Middle Ages.

We shall never know how many men and women took up the ascetic and monastic life in the early Christian centuries. Among the countless thousands for whom the desert became a refuge and place of ultimate spiritual freedom, only relatively few are known by name. The full story of each individual life's adventure remains hidden underneath the testimonials of countless ancient texts, remote to us in time and spirit. But we need to remind ourselves that however difficult it may be to recapture the world of these ascetics and monastics, and however bizarre some of their experiments may appear today, it was among these imperfect seekers of perfection, haunted by the highest ideal, that contemplation and action became closely interwoven, and the foundations of Christian ascetical and mystical theology were laid. The pioneering experiences of these women and men, their journeys of adventure into the unknown, pushed the horizon of the unending quest for God forever further, and created a path which generations of future seekers could follow.

It was not only Christians who did so. There is evidence of Christian influence on the ascetic practices and doctrines of early Islamic mystics. At the time of Mohammed, Christianity was a living force in Arabia, Egypt, North Africa, Nubia, Syria, Asia Minor, in Mesopotamia and

St. Mary of Egypt, by Jusepe de Ribera (1591-1652). Numerous women saints and mystics led deeply devout and exemplary lives. Less often acknowledged than the men, who wrote the official histories of Christian mysticism, these women are of particular interest today when the important contribution of women to the Christian spiritual heritage is becoming much more clearly recognized. (Museo Filangieri, Naples)

Persia, on the shores of the Persian Gulf, in Turkestan, and further East. The rise of Islam did not mean the extermination of Christianity and its adherents. For many centuries Muslims and Christians lived side by side, and there was contact between ascetics and mystics just as there was between traders, craftsmen and scholars. It is evident that at a time when Islamic theological and mystical doctrines were first developed, Muslims found themselves almost everywhere in contact with Christian forms of worship and culture. From a contemporary perspective of interfaith encounter, these contacts would be particularly exciting to explore.

As time moves on, the figures of Christian mysticism become more sharply defined. Of lasting influence for the development of Christian mystical theology, especially in its Greek form in the East, were the three great Cappadocian Fathers, Gregory of Nyssa, his brother Basil the Great, and their friend Gregory of Nazianzus. Cappadocia was an ancient district in east central Anatolia, once under Zoroastrian influence and still retaining an Iranian character when under the power of Rome. This region remained an important bulwark of the East Roman Empire until the eleventh century, and today is part of modern Turkey. Gregory of Nyssa, in particular, was important in the further development of Christian mysticism.

Gregory of Nyssa (330-95)

Gregory came from a distinguished, saintly family in Caesarea Maritima, an ancient port city on the Mediterranean coast, south of contemporary Haifa in Israel, which was then an important center of early Christianity. Deeply influenced by his philosophical training, he first decided to become a teacher of rhetoric. It is uncertain whether or not he was ever married, but it is clear that he eventually took up the life of an ascetic. He then entered the monastery founded by his brother Basil, who had written a well-balanced set of *Long Rules* for his community. These became the basic text for monastic life in the Christian East, and thus exercized an immense influence. They later inspired Benedict of Nursia when he wrote his *Rule* which became foundational for monasticism in the Latin West.

Detail from *St. Antony and St. Paul*, by Mathias Grünewald (1455-1528), from the Isenheim Altarpiece. Male Christian ascetics and mystics often hold a larger place in the Christian imagination than their women contemporaries. Painters have creatively imagined and exoticized some of the experiences of early Christian ascetics. (Unterlinden Museum, Colmar, France)

In Basil's *Rules* practical and spiritual advice go hand in hand. The goal of Christianity is the imitation of Christ, to be practiced according to the vocation of each individual. Everything, whatever it is, is done for the glory of God.

Gregory followed this life of cenobitic monasticism for some years, but at the age of forty he was called to be bishop of Nyssa, a town in Cappadocia. He then became much involved in church affairs, traveled to Jerusalem and Antioch, took part in the Council of Constantinople and was the spokesman of the Orthodox community. The first systematic theological thinker since Origen, Gregory was the leading church theologian in the struggle against Arius, who denied the divinity of Christ. He also was another Christian Platonist, and his brief treatise *On Not Three Gods* relates the theology of three persons in the Godhead— Father, Son, and Spirit—to Plato's teachings on the One and the many.

Gregory's lasting contribution lies in his ascetic and mystical writings which combine Platonic and Christian inspirations. Foremost among them is the *Life of Moses*, written for a friend, but other mystical texts are *From Glory to Glory* and commentaries *On the Beatitudes* and *On The Song of Songs,* all of which combine devotional with ethical interests. Much concerned with the spiritual meaning of biblical texts, Gregory looked to the Old and New Testament and the living tradition of the Alexandrine school to draw inspiration for his teachings. In *The Life of Moses* he used the journey of the ancient Hebrews from Egypt to Mount Sinai as a pattern of the progress of the soul through the temptations of the world to a vision of God. One of the great representatives of the "mysticism of darkness," Gregory was perhaps the first to describe the mystical life as an ascent of the soul to God, an unending journey leading to an ever greater realization of God's ultimate mystery.

In each human soul there exists a divine element, an "inner eye," capable of glimpsing something of God, for there exists a deep relationship, an affinity between human and divine nature. Thus the mind can progress ever further toward the contemplation of God, and yet the more one knows of God, the greater becomes the mystery, the "darkness," the hiddenness of God's face.

Gregory used the events of Moses' life— God's revelation in the burning bush, the reception of the Law on Mount Sinai—to develop his teaching on God as the only One, the Unknowable and Boundless One who transcends everything there is. God became human, so that we can see Him, in Christ.

In Gregory's interpretation, the life of Moses becomes a symbol of the spiritual journey of the Christian to God. Moses's experience was not a withdrawal from active involvement in this world. Although he left the people behind when he "boldly approached the very darkness itself" on Mount Sinai, God instructed him in the cloud. He then sent him down to instruct others and be the leader of his people. The Christian must practice the discipline of the desert, at least inwardly if not outwardly, but ultimately contemplation must flow into action.

Most distinctively, Gregory teaches that spiritual life continually progresses. It is not one of static perfection. Moses's attainments throughout his journey show that from each summit new horizons open, and there is joy in

stored to our original, divine likeness, enabling us to manifest God. Reaching into the infinity of God and entering into ever greater participation in divinity is an unending process.

The life and teaching of Gregory of Nyssa, as that of other early Christian mystics, provide abundant proof that mysticism is not something apart from life and the concerns of the world. On the contrary, the mystical and moral always go together, action and contemplation interact with each other. Christian mystics were ascetics and monastics, but they were also people of their time who shaped the institutions of the Church, influenced poli-

going on and on. "The continual development of life to what is better is the soul's way to perfection." True perfection consists in the growth of ever more goodness by obedience to God in Christ, through whom we shall be re-

tical and economic events, and were involved with the sufferings, pain, and longings of their contemporaries. Their deepest reflections on the meaning of human nature and destiny, however, were fed by the powerful springs of a new faith, which provided a most radiant, all-powerful vision of a God, both far and near, with whom human beings could become united in most profound and intimate love. Such a vision also inspired one of the greatest Christian theologians of the Western Church: St. Augustine.

St. Augustine of Hippo (354-430)

Neoplatonism was the main influence in the development of Christian mysticism in both East and West. After Gregory of Nyssa the transmission of mystical teachings in Eastern Christianity occurred through a different line of teachers from that in the West, where Neoplatonic ideas were handed down for many centuries through Augustine's works. We shall now follow the development of mysticism in the West and return much later to the mystics of Eastern Orthodox Christianity.

Like so many others, Augustine drew on Neoplatonism to explain the gradual rise of the soul away from the distractions of the material world to union with God. His experience, as related in the famous *Confessions*, was the vision of divine light which completely transformed his entire being. After a long and tempestuous quest, he was compelled to recognize that "The true philosopher is the lover of God." In these words from *The City of God* he left a portrait of himself. At first attracted by philosophy and the ideal of contemplation, he eventually became one of the most ardent lovers of God, whose unique religious genius and brilliant intellect have been a lasting inspiration for Christians up to the present.

Who was St. Augustine of Hippo, revered as a doctor of the Church since the early Middle Ages? Applying a modern epithet to him, one might call him both a mystic and a militant. Contemplation and action were mingled in his life as in few others. He told us his absorbing story in his own words in the *Confessions,* the first, and for some the greatest, spiritual autobiography, which he wrote at the age of about forty-five, shortly after he had been made a bishop. It tells the story of his restless, reckless youth, his search and yearning, until he found God and became a Christian. Less factual than devotional, its outpourings speak so much of repentance, thanksgiving, and joy that this book has been described as the "reflections of the bishop on his knees." It has been an immensely influential text, blending mystical insights with personal narrative.

Born in Roman North Africa, Augustine was the son of a Christian mother of great but simple piety, and a pagan father. His mother, later known as St. Monica, instructed him in the Christian faith as best she could, but he abandoned it when he went to study in Carthage. He led a dissipate life and had several mistresses, but eventually lived with one woman for about fifteen years and a son, Adeodatus ("Given by God"), was born from this union.

In Carthage, Augustine studied philosophy and rhetoric, with the ambition of becoming a good speaker. The works of the Roman writer Cicero made an enormous impression on him, lighting in him the desire to seek "the wisdom of eternal truth." He engaged in an intense spiritual struggle to find this truth, and at first he felt enlightened by the teachings of the Manicheans, who taught a dualistic doctrine, believing in a perpetual conflict between the powers of light and darkness. Plotinus taught him to look within

The Vision of St. Augustine, by Vittore Carpaccio (c. 1460-1523). Augustine himself described his mystical vision as happening in a natural setting, by the sea rather than in an enclosed room. This imaginative Renaissance reconstruction is proof of the lasting influence of Augustine's experience, for artists as much as for mystics. (Scuola di San Giorgio degli Schiavoni, Venice)

to find God, and Augustine has described how through an act of introspection he experienced a mystical transformation, a vision or touch, which suddenly made him realize that God is light, a pure, spiritual being, and that evil is darkness, as the Manicheans said. This sudden awareness of God, though moment- ary and fleeting, made him realize that the way of return to God must be through escape from the flesh, which for him meant primarily escape from passionate sexual entanglements.

He left Carthage for Rome, and eventually reached Milan, where he learned much about the heroic achievements of Christian ascetics. He admired the story of St. Antony in the desert and was attracted to the Church through the sermons of St. Ambrose, then Bishop of Milan and a great preacher. Augustine's complete surrender to God is expressed in his immortal conversion story told in Book VIII of the *Confessions*. One day, when walking in a Milan garden, he heard a child's voice calling "take up and read." He opened the New Testament and read the words of St. Paul: "...put on the Lord Jesus Christ and make no provision for the flesh, to gratify its desires"

The Roman ruins of Carthage in Tunisia. The city of Carthage provided a formative influence for the early development of Augustine.

(Rom. 13:14). This broke down his resistance and made him return to the Christianity of his youth.

Soon afterward, in 387, he was baptized by Ambrose in Milan. He then left for Rome, traveling with his mother and some friends. At Ostia, Rome's port city, his mother died, joyous in the knowledge that her son was now a Christian. Augustine left a record of his last conversation with her in a famous discourse in the *Confessions*. This is modeled on the Neo- platonic ascent from this world to the other, and describes a moment- ary experience of eternal life.

In 388, he returned to North Africa, where he stayed in a monastery for several years. A decisive turn came in his life when he was ordained as priest and soon afterwards, in 396, he was made a bishop. From then until his death in 430 he labored ceaselessly for the Church, being deeply involved in all the theological controversies of his time. He wrote on almost all aspects of the Christian faith and produced an immense literary output, made possible only by the constant use of stenographers and his great facility for *ex tempore* formulations.

Augustine's influence on the further development of Christian theology is virtually unparalleled, in that he laid the foundations for the formulation of so many theological doctrines. Yet he has left us no systematic treatise on mysticism. His mystical insights are scattered throughout his writings. Aside from the experiences related in the *Confessions,* some of his deepest thoughts are found in his sermons and scriptural commentaries, especially those on the Psalms, the Gospel and First Letter of St. John, and in his book *De Trinitate.*

Augustine held strong views on the inherently sinful nature of human beings, but also stressed the saving grace and love of God. On one hand he teaches that this grace can be found only through the Church, the city of God on earth, but on the other hand he believes that each soul, however depraved, possesses an inborn relationship with the Absolute, an innate impulse toward God. His mystical theology is theocentric, not Christocentric—it is the passion for the Absolute first experienced in his love for philosophy, for truth and wisdom which grew into the certainty and joy of God's presence whose utter transcendence remains ultimately incommunicable. Augustine was a master in using the language of paradox to express the essentially inexpressible, the knowledge of the Unknowable, the incommunicable joy of divine life.

There is much of the legacy of Platonism in Augustine's longings and search for the truth, in the account of his spiritual journey and encounter with God. But when he eventually turned to biblical religion, he could produce a new and lasting synthesis by combining the classical philosophical heritage with Christian experience and insight. Not only the philosophers, but the Bible also taught that God's image is imprinted on the human soul, and thus the soul provides a temporal and mutable image of the eternal and changeless. It is the task of the human being to seek to know God through this image in the soul. This cannot be achieved, however, without following a disciplined life.

God is the supreme Good. Only in Him can the human being reach perfection. God's nature is love, and by loving God the human being can ultimately participate in divine love, in love itself, which is the empowering source for loving one another. Augustine's all-transforming experience of the dynamic energy and center that is God is beautifully expressed in one of the passages of the *Confessions:*

> Most highest, most good, most potent, most omnipotent; most merciful, yet most just; most hidden, yet most present; most beautiful, yet most strong; stable, yet incomprehensible; unchangeable, yet all-changing; never new, never old; all renewing...ever working, ever at rest; still gathering, yet nothing lacking; supporting, filling and over-spreading; creating, nourishing, and maturing; seeking, yet having all things....
>
> (*Conf.* I:IV,4).

Dionysius the Areopagite, or Pseudo-Dionysius (c. 500)

It was chiefly through Augustine's works that Neoplatonic thought was handed down to Christian theologians in the West, until in the ninth century the works of "Dionysius the Areopagite" were translated into Latin and became widely known in the Church. Dionysius,

Frontispiece of *De Civitate Dei*, Basel, 1490. Augustine was not only a mystic, concerned with the inner experience of the soul, but also a great theological writer whose vision of the city of God influenced the social, political, and ecclesiastical structures of the medieval Christian world. (Bibliothèque des Arts Décoratifs, Paris)

or Denys, in the vernacular, is a mysterious figure. Little is known about this important mystic apart from his works, in which he fused Christian and Greek thought into a synthesis of mystical doctrines which were of seminal influence for all succeeding Christian mystics. They shaped the theology and spirituality of both Eastern Orthodoxy and Western Christianity.

"Dionysius the Areopagite" is a pseudonym, a reference to a convert of St. Paul in Athens, a figure mentioned only briefly in the New Testament (Acts 17:34), and said to be the first bishop of Athens. The mystic who took his name was the author of a series of writings, now thought to be the works of a late fifth- to early sixth-century Syrian monk. His adoption of this pseudonym, with its strong biblical associations, helped his writings to become accepted as authoritative, because of the link with St. Paul. The medieval theologian St. Thomas often refers to Dionysius as an authority in his own works.

It is perhaps particularly appropriate that a writer who speaks so much about the hiddenness of God should remain hidden himself. Four of his treatises and some letters have come down to us, and others are known to be lost. The influence of his writings—*Celestial Hierarchy, Ecclesiastical Hierarchy, Divine Names,* and *Mystical Theology*—on Christian mystical thought can hardly be exaggerated, but it is especially the very short treatise of *Mystical Theology,* consisting of a mere five chapters, which has been more influential than any other.

Denys addresses the most challenging question of how God can be known, or rather, how he can be reached by human beings. He says that God *cannot be known* at all in the ordinary sense, but he can be *experienced,* he can be *reached*

and *found* if he is sought on the right path. *Mystical Theology,* written for his friend Timothy, begins with an invocation of the Trinity, but apart from this there is no mention of God the Father or the Son. The writing focuses entirely on the utter unity of God, the undivided Ultimate Reality and Godhead that lives in complete darkness beyond all light. Dionysius writes that the "unchangeable mysteries of heavenly Truth lie hidden in the dazzling obscurity of the secret Silence, outshining all brilliance with the intensity of their darkness." God is totally beyond the power of the intellect; contemplation is the only way to "divine darkness," which can never be grasped by the human mind.

Like other mystics before him, Dionysius uses the example of Moses in his ascent to Mount Sinai and describes the three stages of the soul's movement to God as those of purification, illumination, and union. This triad is original to Dionysius although he draws on earlier sources, for a similar threefold pattern is already found in Clement of Alexandria, Origen, and Gregory of Nyssa. Later Christian mystical writers derived from this the so-called three ways of mysticism: the purgative, the illuminative, and the unitive.

Dionysius advises his friend not to disclose his teaching to the uninitiated. Those who seek the path of contemplation must leave all activities of the senses and the mind behind. Human thought can deal only with differences and relationships with things that are divided, whereas God is utterly undivided. In Dionysius's illuminating phrase, God must be sought with an "eyeless mind." The soul yearns for that "union with him whom neither being nor understanding can contain," who is "Darkness which is beyond Light", and whose vision can be attained only through the loss of all sight and knowledge.

Sometimes straining his very language to express the use of his negative method to reach that which is beyond all negation, he also gives the example of sculptors at work. These are "men who, carving a statue out of marble, remove all the impediments that hinder the clear perception of the latent image and by this mere removal display the hidden statue itself in its hidden beauty." Similarly the mystic seeker, the soul aiming for vision of the Divine, must remove all impediments so that "ascending upwards from particular to universal conceptions we strip off all qualities in order that we may attain a naked knowledge of that Unknowing which in all existent things is enwrapped by all objects of knowledge, and that we may begin to see that super-essential Darkness which is hidden by all the light that is in existent things." God "plunges the true initiate into the Darkness of Unknowing" where he belongs "wholly to Him who is beyond all things and to no one else" and gains "a knowledge that exceeds understanding." Dionysius also makes affirmations about God. The Godhead overflows into creation "in an unlessened stream into all things that are," but knowing these things is only a knowledge of the shadow, the echo, the reflection of Ultimate Reality, not of the undivided Godhead in itself. He uses this more affirmative approach in his other works to which he refers, such as *Outlines of Divinity* and *Symbolic Divinity*, no longer extant today. In his *Divine Names* he looks at the titles of God drawn from the world of sense, mental and material images, functions and attributes of the Divine. This is a more copious work than *Mystical Theology* because there is so much more to say when affirming something about God. Yet the more the soul soars upwards, the more brevity comes into its own, until the soul is reduced "to absolute dumbness both of speech and thought." Neoplatonism provided Dionysius with the idea of the One of whom nothing can be said as distinct from the manifestations of this One, which can be described. In his mystical theology, Dionysius then combined these ideas by applying both negations and affirmations to one and the same God, thus developing both a theology of denial and affirmation. It is a stark paradox that God reveals something *of* himself—revelations which can be affirmed—yet he does not reveal as he is *in* himself. Thus the soul can reach true knowledge of God in himself only by negating and transcending what he has revealed of himself.

It is a dialectic of affirmation and negation whose goal is the vision of and union with God. But this aim cannot be reached by ourselves; it is achieved by God searching for human beings by the active outreach of his love, his own yearning celebrated in the *Divine Names*. Why is it, Dionysius asks, "that theologians sometimes refer to God as Yearning and Love and sometimes as the yearned-for and the Beloved?" It is because God causes, produces, and generates what is described, and at the same time is this very thing itself. "He is stirred by it and he stirs it. He is moved to it and he moves it." Thus the divine yearning is like traveling in an endless circle "through the Good, from the Good, in the Good and to the Good, unerringly turning, ever on the same center, ever in the same direction, always proceeding, always remaining, always being restored to itself."

Dionysius' mysticism is sometimes criticized for being too individualistic, but his vision of

Atlantis, by Michelangelo (1475-1564). The mystic seeking the presence and power of God, the lineaments of the Divine, is like a sculptor chiseling away at rough stone in search of the shape hidden in the rock. Such is the search for the veiled presence of God in the world, the immense effort and struggle to find the truth, the light, the full glory of the divine vision. (Accademia, Florence)

human union with God cannot be understood without the larger corpus of his writings which describe the community of the Church with its hierarchy, liturgy and sacraments. It is a cosmic and ecclesial vision of great spaciousness, without which his breathtaking mystical vision lacks its wider context and horizon. Some object to the heady Neoplatonism and rarefied abstract thinking of this anonymous writer, but the works of Pseudo-Dionysius came to be accepted as the epitome of apophatic mysticism, or the mysticism of denial with its *via negativa*. Considered as authoritative, his writings greatly stimulated Christian theology and spirituality. They also influenced much of religious life, especially in the cloister, by inspiring a passionate search for God, and leading to the flowering of medieval Christian mysticism.

Orthodox Christian theologians feel somewhat uncomfortable with Dionysius, because of his great emphasis on the Godhead to the detriment of the Trinity. Some think that our own age is perhaps less in tune with Dionysius' apophatic mystical approach because of our more rationalistic theology. But the renewed interest in religious experience, mystical insight, and wisdom across different traditions make the *Mystical Theology* of an unknown ancient author particularly attractive. As Bede Griffith, a twentieth-century Benedictine monk who spent most of his life in India, has said when speaking about contemporary interfaith dialog and the meeting of East and West: "Neoplatonism, as found in Plotinus and later developed by St. Gregory of Nyssa and Dionysius the Areopagite, is the nearest equivalent in the West of the Vedantic tradition of Hinduism in the East."

We shall meet Dionysius and his path of negation in seeking union with God again and again when we look at the great company of Christian mystics who lived during the period usually referred to in the West as the Middle Ages. After the formative period of early Christianity, the Western Church experienced several hundred years, sometimes described as the Dark Ages (seventh to tenth centuries), from which we know little of mystical life until it was renewed in the twelfth century. It is in that century that this story continues.

Cretan icon of the Holy Trinity, seventeenth century. Christian mystical theology is grounded in the three persons of the Trinity, anthropomorphically represented here as Father and Son who hold the world between them and are crowned by the Spirit, embodied in the figure of the dove. (University of Liverpool Art Gallery and Collections, England)

CHAPTER THREE

MEDIEVAL MYSTICS

The Middle Ages are the high point of Christian mysticism. From the early to the late Middle Ages a great company of Christian mystics appeared, some well known, others less so. Beside the great figures were many minor mystics, and new ones continue to be discovered. This is especially true of female mystics, many of whom are becoming known in new ways and are attracting attention more than ever before.

The mystical speculations of Dionysius the Areopagite greatly influenced the Middle Ages and were commented upon by several theologians. In Eastern Christianity it was Maximus the Confessor (580-662) who transmitted the mystical ideas of Dionysius; in the West it was John Scotus Erigena (810-77) who translated his writings into Latin, thus making them available as foundational texts for the mysticism of the Christian West. At first almost forgotten, these translations were rediscovered three centuries later, and thus it happened that from the eleventh to the twelfth century onward mysticism started to flourish in the Western Church. But by and large it remained a mysticism of monastics and celibate clerics.

One of the great mystics of the Christian tradition, and the dominant figure of the twelfth century, is St. Bernard of Clairvaux. The thirteenth century is remembered for the Victorines, who lived in an Augustinian Abbey near Paris and also wrote commentaries on the writings of Dionysius. While Hugh of St. Victor is largely remembered as a theologian, Richard of St. Victor was such a well-known mystic that Dante referred to him in his *Paradiso* (X, 132).

Also very important was Franciscan mysticism. Represented above all by St. Francis of Assisi himself, it is expressed in the writings of the great St. Bonaventure, the *"Doctor Seraphicus,"* who described the soul's mystical ascent to God. Another example of Franciscan mysticism is

Illumination from the Hours of Marguerite d'Orléans, early fourteenth century, showing the Holy Trinity in undivided unity surrounded by the splendors of the created world. (Bibliothèque Nationale, Paris)

found in Angela of Foligno (c.1248-1309), a Franciscan Tertiary, or lay member, of the Order who, after marriage, conversion, and the deaths of her husband, children, and mother, led an ascetic life. During a pilgrimage to Assisi she experienced mystical visions of the Trinity which culminated in the knowledge of "Love Uncreate" and its image in the human soul.

Other great medieval mystics include Hildegard, the famous abbess from Bingen who has become especially well known in recent years. From Italy there are the two Catherines, a hundred years apart, one from Siena, the other from Genoa. In northern Europe we have the women's movement of the Beguines, the Rhineland mystics from Germany and the Netherlands, and the English mystics, male and female, who exercised an important influence on English piety and devotion. All of these have attracted much attention in the twentieth century.

Who were these mystics of a bygone age? How did they seek and describe God, yearn for, desire, and love the Divine, and reach ecstatic union and communion?

The medieval mystic voices are so numerous that it would be impossible to listen to them all. By following the stories of some of the most significant ones we can discover the pattern of their lives, the intensity of their devotion, and the adventure of their encounter with God. They form a story of many parts which begins in the late eleventh century and stretches through to the late fifteenth century. We start with the towering figure of Bernard of Clairvaux, whose life reaches into the middle of the twelfth century.

St. Bernard of Clairvaux (1090-1153)

Bernard was born near Dijon, in France, into a family of seven brothers and one sister of noble stock. Early on he chose the cloister rather than the traditional pursuits of the nobility. In the year 1112, after the death of his parents, he and his brothers entered the austere new Cistercian monastery of Cîteaux, near Dijon, where he pursued his spiritual and theological studies. At that time the return to the primitive rule of St. Benedict and monastic reform spread rapidly throughout Europe. Three years after becoming a

Thirteenth-century manuscript illumination from St. Augustine's Abbey, Canterbury, showing St. Bernard with two pupils at his feet. God's finger pointing from the sky indicates that St. Bernard is writing under divine inspiration and command. (Bodleian Library, Oxford)

Christ Embracing St. Bernard, by Francisco Ribalta (1585-1628). This Spanish painting vividly expresses the deep devotion of St. Bernard for the humanity of Christ. (Prado, Madrid)

monk, Bernard was asked by the Abbot to choose a place for a new monastery, and thus Clairvaux Abbey, near Troyes, in northeastern France, was established.

Bernard became its abbot, and soon made Clairvaux into a major center of the Cistercian Order. Although he was a deeply devoted monk who more than anything else desired a quiet, contemplative life, he became very involved in the Church politics of his time, held offices, founded some sixty monasteries and helped in founding some three hundred others. He could appear obstinate and impetuous, and was given to self-mortification and austerities whose excesses ruined his health; but he became known above all for his saintliness and love of God. He developed a doctrine of mystical love and struggled to combine mystical absorption in God with service to others and the institutional Church.

Bernard held strong orthodox views and was suspicious of secular learning and philosophy in matters of faith. He was not afraid to speak out, denouncing the persecution of the Jews, but helping to condemn Abelard. He is considered the single most important figure of twelfth-century Western Christianity who, through his many writings, exerted an influence over many centuries to come. Canonized in 1174, just over twenty years after his death at Clairvaux, he was much later, in 1820, declared a "Doctor of the Church."

As abbot of the Cistercian Abbey of Clairvaux, Bernard was well known for his deep mystical devotion to the humanity of Christ, especially his childhood and suffering, and his veneration of the Virgin Mary. He was the first to write about the contemplation of the wounds of Christ, one of the great themes of medieval mysticism. His eighty-six sermons on the Song of Songs also express many of his mystical insights, especially about Christ as bridegroom of the soul. His mystical experiences were always linked to a very active life in connection with his work for the Cistercian Order and for the Church of his time.

In his teaching he insisted that prayer, preaching, self-denial, and worship are central to the life of both Church and state, important for monks and lay people alike. God should be loved simply and purely because he is God. Nowhere does this find a more sublime expression than in his short spiritual treatise *De diligendo Deo,* or *On Loving God,* which has been called one of the most outstanding medieval books on mysticism.

Here he describes the ecstasy of the soul transformed into the likeness of God. Written between 1126 and 1141, in response to some questions raised by Haimeric, cardinal deacon and chancellor of the See of Rome, the text contains several major themes connected with the love of God. Loving God means, above all, to love without measure, but it is also linked to humility and obedience to God's will

Bernard's clear and orderly mind sets out the different reasons for and the several degrees of this exalted love. Why should human beings love God above all? Bernard lists three reasons: we should love God because of God's gift of himself to us, because of the gifts of nature, and because of the gift of ourselves. The whole of spiritual life

St. Bernard, Abbot of Clairvaux, an illumination from the Hours of Etienne Chevalier, c. 1445. Here we see the powerful teaching authority that Bernard exercized over the Cistercian Order. The lower panel shows the devil attempting to distract him from following his vocation. (Musée Condé, Chantilly, France)

The mystical union of the soul. An illumination from the Rothschild Canticles showing the soul as Bride of Christ in the mystical bedchamber, filled with visionary ecstasy. Christ the Bridegroom descends from heaven and enters the world as a dramatic sunburst. (Beinecke Library, Yale University Library, New Haven, Ct.)

sincere because it does not seek its own advantage. "Tasting God's sweetness entices us more to pure love than does the urgency of our own needs," Bernard writes. This is how he describes this highest experience:

To lose yourself, as if you no longer existed, to cease completely to experience yourself, to reduce yourself to nothing is not a human sentiment but a divine experience....

It is deifying to go through such an experience. As a drop of water seems to disappear completely in a big quantity of wine, even assuming the wine's taste and color, just as red, molten iron becomes so much like fire it seems to lose its primary state; just as the air on a sunny day seems transformed into a sunshine instead of being lit up; so it is necessary for the saints that all human feelings melt in a mysterious way and flow into the will of God. Otherwise, how will God be all in all if something human survives in man?

At other times, Bernard appeals to the imagery of the Song of Songs and speaks of Christ as the bridegroom coming into the soul. He comes without being seen or heard, from without and within, from the highest parts and the deepest depths of the soul, stretching farther than Bernard could see and yet being utterly inward, so that he can affirm with St. Paul that "In Him we live and move and have our being." He speaks of Christ's wisdom, his gentleness and kindness, his renewal of spirit and mind. Bernard expresses his wondrous amazement that in his inmost being "I have beheld to some degree the beauty of His glory and have been filled with awe as I gazed at His manifold greatness."

is seen as a response to God's gratuitous love.

If we know ourselves, we are already on the way to God, because God created us in the divine image. But we cannot find God unless we have first been found and led by him so that we desire to seek him more. Bernard distinguishes carnal and social love, love of self and love of others, and divides love into four degrees. First we love ourselves for our own sake; then we love God, but for our own sake. Then come our love of God for his sake, and, the highest degree, our love of ourselves for God's sake. This divine love is

The Abbey of St. Victor, outside Paris, was a great center of learning. It was in such monastic houses that much of Christian mysticism flourished in medieval Europe. Detail from plans for the tapestry, early sixteenth century. (Bibliothèque Historique de la Ville de Paris)

One of Bernard's favorite themes was the wisdom of God which builds herself a house in Mary and each Christian. Mary, the symbol of feminine qualities *par excellence*, is highly exalted in Bernard's works, especially in his *Homilies in Praise of the Virgin Mother*. What is most interesting to us are Bernard's view that both feminine and masculine qualities can be legitimately applied to God—and some writers have even compared his views to Jungian theory—and his emphasis on the necessity of the feminine in the work of salvation.

Richard of St. Victor (c. 1120–73)

One of Bernard's friends and the most famous teacher of his day was William of Champeaux. He founded the Augustinian Abbey of St. Victor near Paris in 1113, which developed into a famous center of medieval philosophy, theology, and mysticism. While its monks were no less intent than Bernard on fostering mystical contemplation, they did not mistrust secular learning as he did, but cultivated the liberal arts and classical philosophy as an aid to mystical contemplation. The Abbey thus produced a number of prominent scholars, mystics and poets of whom we shall mention only Richard of St. Victor, who

Diagram of the Temple at Jerusalem from Richard of St. Victor's Commentary on Ezekiel. Medieval mystics and painters imagined the Jewish Temple as a Romanesque building, with storeys as stages of ascent to God. (Bodleian Library, Oxford)

was Prior of the Abbey from 1162 until his death in 1173.

A Scot by birth, Richard was steeped in philosophy but dedicated himself above all to contemplation, or what we now call mysticism. Not unlike Bernard, he speaks of the *Four Degrees of Burning Love,* as one of his writings is entitled. But his best known texts are the so-called *Benjamin Minor,* or *The Preparation of the Soul,* and *Benjamin Major,* or *Contemplation,* titles which are based on his allegorical reference to Jacob's twelve sons, each of whom personifies one of the virtues. Benjamin, the youngest, stands for contemplation, and for this reason these two important texts on mysticism came to be called *Benjamin Minor* and *Benjamin Major* after the Middle Ages.

Richard of St. Victor was the first theologian to attempt a systematic treatment of mystical theology. His works exercised a wide influence on both contemporary and subsequent medieval writers. He was also the first medieval mystic to apply systematic psychology to the mystical experience when he describes the ascent of the mind from the contemplation of visible to invisible things and ultimately to a final transforming union. The ultimate state is one of utter self-surrender and ecstasy which, however, must make the soul return to compassionate work in the world in imitation of Christ.

Richard follows the Augustinian tradition in seeing knowledge of God as an ascent. The human mind is active in thinking, meditation and contemplation. Whereas the activity of thinking remains largely undisciplined, however, meditation requires a sustained mental effort, and contemplation takes the mind beyond the reach of reason to a state of ecstatic "alienation" outside and beyond itself. Ecstasy takes place when the soul has ascended to the point where it has left behind both imagination and reason. Richard speaks of the "wedding" of the human with the divine spirit, implying a state of complete self surrender. In describing the ecstasy of the human mind, he relates it to three causes:

For it comes to pass that sometimes through greatness of devotion, or great wonder, or exceeding exultation, the mind cannot possess itself in any way, and being lifted up above itself, passes into ecstasy. The human mind is raised above itself by the greatness of its devotion, when it is kindled with such fire of heavenly desire that the flame of inner love flares up beyond human bearing.

In such a state the human soul is "radiant with infused heavenly light and lost in wonder at the supreme beauty of God" and "torn from the foundation of her being" so that she "no longer thirsts *for* God, but *into* God." But what should those feel who have never experienced such ecstasy? Are they not loved? Do they perhaps not love to the highest degree? Richard assures his reader:

Whoever you are, if you loved fully and perfectly perhaps the perfection of your love, the urge of your burning desire would carry you away into this kind of ecstasy …if you were truly worthy of divine love, perhaps he would enlighten the eyes of your intelligence so greatly with the effulgence of his light and inebriate the desire of your heart with such a taste of his intimate sweetness, that thereby he would carry you up above yourself and lift you up to divine things by ecstasy…

But God's presence, the sublime fruit of contemplation, is not enough on its own. It is further surpassed by a higher, "fourth degree of love," whereby the soul withdraws from its annihilation and is raised in Christ, following his example and "bringing forth its children" through compassionate work in the world. Like all Christian mystics, Richard's understanding of mysticism is that it is not centered solely on the soul's enjoyment of God, but that it becomes fecund in the world. Richard of St. Victor thus combined the affirmative way of mysticism with the negative methods advocated by Dionysius the Areopagite.

Dante refers to Richard in his *Paradiso* (X, 132) as "In contemplation more than a man." Richard's synthesis of Augustinian and Dionysian elements, combined with his interest in the experiential psychology of the spiritual life and his careful analysis of the different stages of contemplation, no doubt provided many contemplatives with the framework for their spiritual quest. It is thus not surprising that the works of Richard of St. Victor were widely read during the Middle Ages, in France, England, Germany, and Spain. Directly or indirectly, they influenced most later spiritual writers in the Christian West.

Medieval mysticism was not only linked to the monasticism of the cloister. Important new elements were introduced into religious and spiritual life through extra-monastic developments. It was above all the figure of St. Francis and his radical mentality in imitating the poverty of Christ in a literal sense which led to a new sensibility and intense devotion to the presence of God within all created beings, a perspective which highlighted the importance and interdependence of humanity and the world of nature.

St. Francis of Assisi (1181-1226)

This great charismatic and Christ-like figure of utter humility and simplicity created a new spiritual consciousness in the Christian West. Although he left few writings, his sense of God's all-pervading presence, his freshness of vision and his intensive love for all God's creatures, great and small, human and animal, gave the Church an important spiritual legacy which has attracted attention over and over again, not least in the new movement of creation spirituality in our own time.

Whereas earlier medieval mystics pursued their flight from the world and its burdens by seeking the stability of monastic life, such flight into perfection was now sought in the instability of life on the road, in pilgrimages and crusades, so that St. Francis addressed his brethren as "pilgrims and strangers."

Until the age of twenty, Francesco Bernardone lived the life of the son of a rich cloth merchant in the Italian town of Assisi, helping his father in business. Then in 1202, during a border dispute with a neighboring town, he was taken prisoner and held captive for some months. After his release he suffered a serious illness, during which he became dissatisfied with his worldly life. He underwent an inner conversion and from that time on devoted himself to a life of prayer and service to the poor.

During a pilgrimage to Rome he was moved by the beggars outside St. Peter's and exchanged his clothes with one of them, spending a day begging for alms himself. This experience affected him deeply, and on his return to Assisi he decided to minister to lepers and repair the ruined church of St. Damiano, which led his father to disown him. One morning in church, Francis heard the words of the Gospel in which Jesus asks his disciples to leave everything in order to follow him. Francis understood this as a personal call, discarded his belongings, put on a long, dark garment girded with a cord, and set out to save souls. Before long he gathered a band of like-minded followers devoted to a life of poverty, compassionate service, and preaching of the Gospel. Soon he drew up a simple rule of life for himself and his followers, and this was the beginning of the Franciscan Order.

These ideals were equally attractive to a young noblewoman of Assisi, Clara, or Clare, who took Francis as her spiritual teacher and guide, and founded a similar order for women, centered on the church of St. Damiano in Assisi. Clare became a nun in 1212. She outlived Francis

St. Francis Receiving the Stigmata, by Giotto (c. 1266-1337). Toward the end of his life, when living on Mount Alvernia in the Apennines, St. Francis's culminating mystical experience was a glorious vision of the crucified Christ, who impressed on Francis's body the marks of his own wounds, the stigmata. (Louvre, Paris)

by many years, remaining always faithful to his vision of poverty, mutual love, and shared contemplation of "the Lord who was poor as he lay in the crib, poor as he lived in the world, who remained naked on the cross," as Francis wrote in his *Testament*. There was a deep spiritual friendship between her and Francis which was based on the love and veneration of the humanity and poverty of Christ.

Setting up his order, negotiating with and befriending several ecclesiastical figures of his time, together with his various travels, made Francis's life eventful. In 1214-15 he visited the south of France and Spain with the intention of converting the Moors to Christianity. Illness prevented him from reaching Africa, but in 1219 he undertook another preaching tour to Eastern Europe and Egypt.

Francis identified his whole life and that of his brothers as "the life of the Gospel of Jesus Christ." Consumed by the consciousness of God's all-pervading presence and purpose, he saw everybody as a child of God and craved to know the uncreated Father through all of creation, especially through the humanity of his Son.

Towards the end of his life Francis retired to a hermitage at Mount Alvernia in the Apennines, where in September 1224 he fasted for

Fifteenth-century painting of St. Clare by A. and B. Vivarini. This panel from the church of St. Francesco in Padua is now in the Kunsthistorisches Museum, Vienna.

weeks and contemplated Christ's sufferings. After an entire night spent in prayer, as the sun rose in the morning, he had a glorious vision of a crucified seraph with six outspread wings. Stirred to his depths, he felt sharp stings mingled with ecstasy and it was then that he received the *stigmata*, the impression of the five wounds of Christ crucified, on his own body. This experience is well testified by several thirteenth-century sources and left a deep impression on the medieval mind.

Shortly afterwards Francis composed his great *Canticle of Brother Sun*, a poetic hymn in praise of the Most High by a man fully at peace, in harmony with the whole cosmos, to whom all elements are brothers and sisters. Well known, too, is his prayer "Lord, make me an instrument of your peace. Where there is hatred, let me sow love….O Divine Master, grant that I may not so much seek to be consoled as to console…to be loved as to love…."

In comparison with other mystics Francis left few writings. His mystical spirituality lives on through the example of his life; it is found in his simple faith, his passionate devotion to God and human beings, his love of nature, and his deep humility. The greatness of this man was immediately recognized by the Church,

St. Francis's love and care for all living creatures introduced a new attitude towards nature into Christian devotional and mystical practice.

which made him a saint in 1228, two years after his death. His inspiring example also lived on in the Franciscan Order, whose conflicts had already begun during Francis's lifetime. It became subdivided and developed into several branches, but all of them were inspired by the great figure of their founder, one of the most cherished saints of the Christian Church. His example determined the shape of Franciscan spirituality which later contributed several popular devotional practices to Christianity, such as the Christmas crib, the Stations of the Cross, and possibly the Angelus, also known as the "Ave Maria." All of these directly relate to and celebrate the humanity of Christ.

Soon after Francis's death, the stories associated with his life were collected together and several Lives were written. In 1266 the Franciscan Order officially authorized the *Legenda Major*, the Life written by St. Bonaventure, and ordered the suppression of all others. This led to the growth of oral legends which culminated in the classic collection of the *Fioretti*, the *Little Flowers of St. Francis*, a widely read and much loved book.

We shall now turn to the great Franciscan

mystical theologian St. Bonaventure, who lived shortly after St. Francis.

St. Bonaventure (1221-74)

Born near Viterbo in central Italy, Bonaventure studied at the University of Paris and subsequently became a professor of theology there. In 1242 he entered the Franciscan Order of which he was made head, or minister general, in 1257. Later still he became a bishop and cardinal. As such he played a significant part at the Council of Lyons in 1274, which was still sitting when he died. He left a considerable body of writings, including commentaries on the Scriptures, but he was most influential through his mystical theology which he set forth in his *Itinerarium Mentis in Deum* or *The Mind's Journey to God*, his greatest speculative and mystical work.

Following in the footsteps of St. Francis, Bonaventure tells how, shortly after becoming minister general and thirty-three years after the death of his founder, he ascended Mount Alvernia to meditate in the place where St. Francis had experienced the miraculous vision of the crucified seraph. While there, Bonaventure was blessed with the same vision of a six-winged angel, whose three pairs of wings came to symbolize for him the three major phases of the soul's ascent to God. He recounts this extraordinary experience in the prologue of his *Itinerarium,* to which he gave the subtitle "The Mendicant's Vision in the Wilderness." It is because of this vision of the seraph that St. Bonaventure was later called "The Seraphic Doctor."

It is through this mystical theology that Bonaventure provides his spiritual instruction, which is centered on the unifying experience of divine illumination. He holds an essentially mystical theory of knowledge which follows the Augustinian tradition. This made him less interested in the new Aristotelian doctrines, which became known at that time and are chiefly associated with the theology of St. Thomas of Aquinas.

For Bonaventure, contemplation is both the goal and the journey. The spiritual allegory of the seraph with six wings grouped in three pairs symbolizes the three major phases of illumination in the soul's ascent to God. Prayer is vitally important in this, and divine help comes to those who seek the knowledge needed for the ascent.

The first pair of stages involves reflecting on the sensible, corporeal world which is a ladder for ascending to God. The world bears traces of God's hand, so that we can recognize his creative power in it. We understand God *through* sensible things, but we also see God *in* sensible things as essence, potency, and presence.

In the second pair of stages, understanding is gained by entering our own minds and taking them as objects of our reflection. We can see God's image stamped upon our natural powers of memory, intellect, and choice. For Bonaventure, memory, intelligence, and will reflect the Trinity of "Father, Word, and Love," and the soul in the "trinity of its powers" is seen as being created in the image of God. After having learned the *way* of God through contemplating the world, the awareness of the *truth* of God is gained through and in our own minds.

The third and final pair of the ascent occurs when our minds turn to what is "eternal, most

The celestial hierarchy of Seraphim, Cherubim, and Saints, painted on the ceiling of the cathedral in Cefalu, Sicily. The six-winged Seraphim, first described in a vision of the prophet Isaiah, are angels close to the glory of God's throne, especially praised for the burning fervor of their love.

spiritual and above us," the first principle of being or God himself. By reflecting on pure being, we know God as unity; by reflecting on the goodness of pure being, we know God as Trinity.

The six stages of ascent correspond to the six stages of the soul's powers through which the ascent is made: sense, imagination, reason, intellect, intelligence, and the illumination of conscience. The final, ultimate goal beyond the six stages is not within the soul's power to reach. It is given as a gift: a seventh stage of repose and illumination by supreme wisdom made possible through Christ as mediator. It is a stage of mental and mystical elevation in which all intellectual operations cease, a unifying experience of divine illumination which is "mystical and most secret, which no man knows but he that has received it." Bonaventure cannot say more than:

If you should ask how these things come about, question grace, not instruction; desire, not intellect; the cry of prayer, not pursuit of study; the spouse, not the teacher; God, not man; darkness, not clarity; not light, but the wholly flaming fire which will bear you aloft to God with fullest unction and burning affection.

This is a mysticism of a fundamentally Christocentric emphasis, also expressed through Bonaventure's devotion to the Sacred Heart, as when he writes: "Behold, I have one heart with Jesus." Influenced by Gregory of Nyssa and Dionysius the Areopagite, it is a mysticism of

darkness expressed through the classic threefold way of purgation, illumination, and union.

Franciscan devotion to the humanity and passion of the crucified Christ expressed itself in a rich heritage of spiritual and mystical writing. Franciscan wisdom touches on the heart of human, cosmic, and divine reality. Entering into the poverty of the cross of Jesus is to know and find there the compassionate wisdom of God from within God. In one of his sermons on the nativity Bonaventure describes this wisdom as a union in which "immensity is tempered by smallness; strength by weakness; clarity by obscurity; immortality by mortality; divinity by humanity; and riches by poverty."

Somewhat akin to Bonaventure's own spiritual journey are the visions of the **Blessed Angela of Foligno** (1248-1309). A penitent widow from Umbria, she joined the Third Order of the Franciscans which grouped together lay followers of St. Francis. Her journey of intense spiritual experience, linked to frequent visions of Christ's passion, is preserved in a writing called *Memorial,* which divides the spiritual ascent to God into thirty different steps.

It is impossible to describe these here in detail, but with the cross as her inspiration she discovered new abilities to see, taste, feel, and smell, and was able to return Christ's love to her by fervently loving the crucified Christ. She experienced the cross from within as she entered into the experience of Christ, his absolute poverty and helplessness on the cross, which led her into a "most horrible darkness" and suffering. Through following and embracing Christ crucified, she participated in the complete self-emptying of Christ on the cross and thereby found a radically new experience of God,

Detail from *The Vision of the Blessed Angela of Foligno,* from the monastery of the Contesse Foligno in Perugia, Italy. The mural shows her receiving sustenance from an angel and blessings from the hand of God.

touching the uncreated All-Good, which is darkness to the limited human mind.

Evelyn Underhill, the well-known writer on mysticism, considers Angela of Foligno as "in many respects the most remarkable of the great Franciscan mystics," but we shall leave her to look at three other, quite different women mystics who are generally better known and belong to different centuries.

Hildegard of Bingen (1098-1179)

The great mystical visionary Hildegard was a poet, musician and painter, and the first major German mystic. She left us a substantial body of writings on nature and medieval medicine and, above all, her major work *Scivias*, or *Know the Ways*, whose visions are accompanied by striking, colorful miniatures. The end of the book is a drama set to music which describes the eternal battle between good and evil. It has been described as the earliest morality play yet discovered. With such great creative achievements it is no surprise that Hildegard is sometimes compared to such visionary writers as Dante and Blake. Her works are now enjoying a great revival, although earlier writers on mysticism paid little attention to them.

Hildegard was the tenth and youngest child of a noble German family. When she was eight, her parents entrusted her for education to the recluse Jutta von Spanheim, who raised her, and she later decided to take vows and follow the Benedictine way of life. After Jutta's death she was elected as the new abbess of her convent, which soon moved to Rupertsberg, near Bingen, on the Rhine.

Hildegard had been a spiritually precocious child who experienced mystical visions from a young age to the end of her life. For her, God was the living light, the *lux vivens*. She describes her visions in terms of light, speaks of mystical rapture and prophecies and expresses her passionate desire for God with great intensity. Her visions are marked by brilliant colors, her descriptions by apophatic negations.

Because of the vivid apocalyptic visions of her prophecies, Hildegard is sometimes referred to as the "Sibyl of the Rhine." It seems that she always had poor physical health and suffered psychosomatic troubles. It has been suggested that many of her visions were related to migraine attacks. Yet she was a woman of indomitable energy and great strength who founded two convents, undertook a great deal of travelling and preaching, and dictated her works to a scribe, the monk Volmar. Her second abbey, Eibingen, near Rüdesheim, became the center of Hildegardian reform and renewal.

Hildegard produced a trilogy of visionary books of which the first, *Scivias*, is the most important. In 1141, when she was "forty-two years and seven months old," she received a disturbing vision from God with the commandment, "Write what you see and hear!" She began, and took more than ten years to complete the work. At first she was hesitant and sought advice, not least from her near contemporary Bernard of Clairvaux, who encouraged her and influenced the Pope to give his approbation to this female prophet.

Scivias is a complex book which has been

Hildegard's powerful visions described in her book *Scivias* include both figurative and abstract images. Here the divine energy runs like fire through the mystic circle. (Abbey of St. Hildegard, Rüdesheim, Germany)

Nineteenth-century engraving of Hildegard of Bingen. The great prophetic voice of Hildegard exercised a powerful influence through her writing, her preaching, her dramatic work and her music. In recent years she has attracted much renewed interest.

I, the fiery life of divine essence, am aflame beyond the beauty of the meadows. I gleam in the waters. I burn in the sun, moon, and stars. With every breeze, as with invisible life that contains everything, I awaken everything to life. I am the breeze that nurtures all things green. I encourage blossoms to flourish with ripening fruits. I am the rain coming from the dew that causes the grasses to laugh with the joy of life.

Hildegard's thought is holistic and healing; it celebrates the cosmos and seeks compassion, peace, and justice. For her, wisdom is less about thinking than tasting. In Latin, wisdom (*sapientia*) and taste (*sapere*) are words stemming from the same root. To build the house of wisdom in ourselves and in our community means to learn the art of savoring and the joy of living.

Hildegard's struggle for wisdom was gained at the cost of great physical and spiritual pain. We can discern in her works the immense effort to break free from traditional patterns and create something new. Though still constrained by the feudal structures of her time, Hildegard brought forth a universal vision of extraordinary power and inspiration. Her visions are not exclusive, but wholly inclusive. The work entrusted by God to humankind has to be carried out by man and woman together, and she includes the feminine element in her understanding of God, for God's love is above all a maternal, life-giving love.

The extraordinary richness, prophetic power, and great mystical unity of Hildegard's visionary creations are being drawn upon only now, when the threat to our environment makes us seek new spiritual resources for nurturing a deeply reverential attitude to the sacredness of all life. Hildegard challenged the clergy and lay

described as an encyclopedia of salvation. Divided into three parts, it describes twenty-six visions in all, accompanied by thirty-six miniatures. One of Hildegard's major themes is the search for wisdom, that "elusive treasure" which dwells "wonderfully in the Godhead's heart," and which we have to recover as our "original wisdom." Wisdom is cosmic too, as the keeper of order and justice. Wisdom is compassion, and Christ, the incarnation of God's compassion, is also the incarnation of God's wisdom. Wisdom is deeply involved in the ongoing work of creation:

people of her time; the ecstatic nature of her writings, paintings, and music are challenging us now, but in a new way.

It is said that on September 17, 1179, two streams of light appeared in the sky and formed a cross over the room where Hildegard lay dying. While the visions of her lifetime had come to her from the "living light," her death made her enter the eternal light, an event marked by a vision visible to all.

Hildegard is the first great woman mystic from Northern Europe that we have encountered so far, but we shall meet several more later. We shall now turn back to Italy, to tell the story of the two Catherines who, each in her own way, so well combined the contemplative and the active life.

St. Catherine of Siena (1347-80)

During the fourteenth and fifteenth centuries, Italy produced a rich spiritual literature, full of mystical devotion and religious fervor. Several of its works come from female mystics, of whom Catherine of Siena is perhaps the best known.

Born into the family of a dyer in the district of Siena, Caterina Benincasa was the twenty-fourth of twenty-five children. Influenced by the austerities of the desert fathers, she took a vow of virginity at the age of seven and became a Dominican Tertiary at the age of sixteen. That meant that she was a lay member of the order, bound by simple vows but living outside the convent. She soon gained a reputation for her great holiness and severe asceticism. From early on she experienced visions, ecstasies, and spiritual struggles which culminated in 1366, when she was not yet twenty, in her "mystical marriage with Christ," so beautifully depicted in several Renaissance paintings.

This experience showed her the need to go out into the world and help her neighbors out of love for God. Thus she was not only an ascetic and mystic, but also an activist, always motivated by God's love for the human being, about which she said: "Nails would not have held the God-man fast to the cross, had not love held him there."

She devoted herself with such dedication to the sick and poor of Siena that they called her "our Holy Mother." Her guiding thought was that "there is no perfect virtue—none that bears fruit —unless it is exercised by means of our neighbor." Her public ministry also involved great concern for the Church, which she understood as the kingdom of God on earth. She first worked for peace when Florence was placed under an interdict because it was in arms against the Pope, Gregory XI. This made her travel to Avignon to plead with the Pope on behalf of the city, but also to persuade him to return to Rome. Later when the Great Schism of the Papacy broke out, she became an active supporter of Pope Urban VI, urging bishops and monarchs in many letters to return to his obedience. Thus she played an active part in the ecclesiastical politics of her day. She wrote to the Pope himself, reminding him that care for spiritual things stood above things temporal. By the time she died, she was greatly exhausted from her public life and the sacrifices she had made. But her public ministry ultimately derived its strength and authority from her intense spiritual experiences, which were recognized by others.

She had an extraordinary devotion to the Precious Blood, the blood of Christ shed during

The Mystic Marriage of St. Catherine, Florentine School, fifteenth century. Catherine of Siena took a vow of virginity at a very young age, and the story of her inner life culminated in a mystical marriage to Christ. This event is symbolized here, with the infant Jesus putting a ring on her finger. (Museo di San Marco dell'Angelico, Florence)

St. Catherine of Siena, by Giovanni-Battista Tiepolo (c. 1746). Catherine had a deep devotion to the suffering Christ and, like St. Francis, she received the marks of his wounds, the stigmata, on her own body. Here she is depicted, almost Christlike, with a crown of thorns on her head. (Kunsthistorisches Museum, Vienna)

his passion. Devotion to this blood, especially in connection with the eucharist, and belief in its redeeming power go back to the early Christian centuries. The great intensity of her mystical devotion and trances produced, as with St. Francis, the physical imprinting of the stigmata, the five wounds of Christ on her body, which she described in the following words: "I saw the crucified Lord coming down to me in a great light…Then from the marks of His most sacred wounds I saw five blood-red rays coming down upon me, which were directed towards the hands and feet and heart of my body. Wherefore, perceiving the mystery, I straight-away exclaimed, 'Ah! Lord, my God, I beseech Thee, let not the marks appear outwardly on the body.'…So great is the pain that I endure sensibly in all those five places, but especially within my heart, that unless the Lord works a new miracle, it seems not possible to me that the life of my body can stay with such agony."

The record of her mystical experiences is found in her book *Dialogo*, her dialog with God, which she dictated as she did all her writings. It illustrates her view of the "inner cell" where the knowledge of God and of the self is found. Speaking movingly of her experience of God she writes: "The more I enter, the more I find, and the more I find the more I seek of Thee. Thou art the Food that never satiates, for when the soul is satiated in Thine abyss it is not satiated, but ever continues to hunger and thirst for Thee."

Much of the book was dictated when Catherine was in a state of ecstasy. Its central message is that love is the way to perfection, and the heart of the book describes Christ as the bridge which must be crossed, from earth to

The Fainting of St. Catherine, by Il Sodoma (1477-1549). Catherine of Siena is seen here falling to her knees in pain and being supported by her friends. Her insight into the agony of Christ was expressed through her veneration of the precious blood, shed during his passion. (San Domenico, Siena)

heaven, by those who would find God. The bridge is built of the stones of true and sincere virtues, and on it is an inn where food is given to the travelers. Those who cross the bridge go to eternal life; those who go underneath it find everlasting death.

Soon after her death, Catherine of Siena was recognized as a saint, but it was only in 1939 that she was declared the patron saint of Italy, and more recently still, in 1970, that she was proclaimed a "Doctor of the Church," a title very few women hold.

St. Catherine of Genoa (1447-1510)

Catherine came from the famous Fieschi family in Genoa, where she received a careful and sound education as befitted her noble status. Her early aspirations to become a nun were frustrated by her relatives when, for political reasons, they married her at the age of sixteen to a young man, Guiliano Adorno, who was worldly, pleasure-loving, and indulgent. Catherine experienced considerable unhappiness and spent some sorrowful years in seclusion until she was able to free herself from her husband. She then devoted herself to prayer, contemplation, and strict discipline. In 1473 she underwent a deep mystical experience marked by close union with God. From now on her life was transformed. She reached great spiritual heights, but balanced ascetic discipline with an active life of service to the ill and poor.

She founded the first hospital in Genoa, where she gave such selfless service that her husband was eventually converted and assisted her in her care of the sick. He later became a Franciscan Tertiary, but Catherine herself never joined an order. Her devotion to the eucharist was so intense that from 1475 onwards she received communion almost daily, a practice extremely rare in the Middle Ages for those other than priests.

Soon she gathered around her a band of devoted friends and followers to whom she described her mystical experiences in conversations between 1499 and 1507. These accounts were given a literary form, probably not by Catherine herself, and published only much later, in 1551, as *Vita e dottrina*. This work forms the basis for two separately published books, *Dialogues on the Soul and the Body* and *Treatise on Purgatory*. In the early twentieth century, attention was drawn to Catherine's remarkable mystical, mental, and at times almost pathological experiences through the classic study by Baron Friedrich von Hügel, *The Mystical Element in Religion as Studied in Saint Catherine of Genoa and Her Friends* (1908).

The last ten years of Catherine's life were marked by violent interior emotions, mentioned in her works. It has been said that in many ways Catherine of Genoa is a "theologian of purgatory," a purgatory which she herself experienced in a marriage she did not desire, in her care for plague victims, and also in her nervous illness. She also experienced purgatory spiritually, as the soul's realization of its own imperfections, in her search for salvation and purification.

Influenced by Plato and Dionysius, the focus of her mysticism was, in spite of her eucharistic devotion, not so much Christ, but above all the infinite God. Her mysticism is primarily theocentric, not Christocentric. She speaks of the absorption into the totality of God as if immersed into an ocean: "I am so…submerged in His immense love, that I seem as though immersed in the sea, and nowhere able to touch, see or feel aught but water." At the height of her mystical experiences she could exclaim: "My being is God, not by simple participation but by a true transformation of my being."

Catherine of Genoa was beatified in 1737, and in 1944 Pope Pius XII proclaimed her Patroness of the Hospitals in Italy. Unlike her predecessor Catherine of Siena, she did not become involved with the political concerns of

The Hospital of St. Matthew, by Jacopo da Pontormo (1494-1556). Catherine of Genoa founded the first hospital in her native city. The devotion of medieval mystics to the human suffering of Christ often resulted in an active engagement with the world, leading to practical help for the poor and ill. (Accademia, Florence)

her time. Neither the fall of Constantinople in 1453, which had considerable repercussions on the city of Genoa, nor the historic landing of her townsman Columbus in America in 1498, find any mention in her works. Her entire attention was devoted to her charitable works and to her circle of women friends who may well have been responsible for putting her personal teachings into literary form and getting them published. We know little about this group of women surrounding Catherine, but we have far more information about the female mystics living in northern Europe, the Beguines.

The Beguines

Until the recent revival of interest caused by the women's movement, the work of medieval female mystics had for a long time remained a neglected part of the Christian mystical heritage. Yet between the twelfth and the fourteenth centuries we can observe a significant increase of women's participation in the religious life, with a strong emphasis on mystical and para-mystical phenomena. The different life patterns of medieval men and women also led to a noticeable contrast between lay female saints and clerical male saints.

Women's spirituality reflects the importance of affectivity—of body and feeling—and many spiritual themes are gender-specific. Female saints have been called "models of suffering" in contrast to male "models of action." Women's writing was less grounded in theological training than men's; it was more affective, experiential, and devotional, with an emphasis on Christ's suffering humanity and the eucharist—God was both mother and father, "judge" and "nurse" to human souls.

Of particular richness is the neglected heritage of the Beguines, lay women, who lived an ideal of Christian spirituality in self-suffi-cient communities in differ-ent parts of Europe. Their groups spread from the Low Countries along the Rhine valley to Germany and France, even to England, and given their independence and self-sufficiency, they have been called "feminists before their time." A much smaller, parallel, male lay movement, the Beghards, also came into existence. These women and men were considered by many of their contemporaries as the most devout Christians of their age.

The Beguines formed their own settlements, the *beguinages* (of which some are still in existence in the Netherlands and Belgium), which consisted of many different houses and sometimes also a church, cemetery, hospital, brewery, public square, and streets. The city of Cologne is said to have had a total of a hundred Beguine houses, holding a thousand women, between 1250 and 1350, whereas Strasbourg housed some six hundred Beguines in the fifteenth century—figures which attest to the popularity of the movement at that time.

These pious women followed a spiritual vocation of their own choosing, forming a movement of *mulieres indisciplinatae*, women who lived without a religious rule. They lived singly, but also grouped themselves under the guidance of a *magistra*, or "mistress," whereas a priest, also known as "master," gave spiritual direction.

Thus the movement developed some kind of pattern, and later still Beguines came to live together in an enclosure in a special district of a town, developing their own rule. Eventually the more populated enclosures with their church and other institutions grew into an independent parish of the town, with small houses for one or two Beguines, communal houses for small

This wandering mendicant, possibly a Beghard, is characteristic of the late medieval movement of lay devotion. This was much practiced by women, the Beguines, many of whom became important mystical figures.

groups of women, the house of the Grand Mistress, the guest house, where visitors stayed and where the old and sick were cared for, and alms houses for poor Beguines. It was a whole world of its own which could serve as a place of refuge for those in need of help and advice. One can still sense something of the spirit of such places today when visiting the well-known "Princely Beguinage" in Bruges.

Among the Beguines were many mystics and visionaries, who wrote stirring mystical poetry about their love of God, but also about the humanity and passion of Christ. Women were rarely allowed to preach, but they felt compelled by God to write and communicate their powerful inner experiences. The Beguines preferred vernacular language to Latin, and adopted the courtly love lyric for their mystical poetry. Rather than just writing about God, they described the relationship of the soul to God in autobiographical form and used highly charged, erotic images to convey their own relationship with God. Many of the expressions of their mystical experiences and insights influenced the much better-known male Rhineland mystics. Because of their lyrical love mysticism, expressed in songs and poetry, these female mystics have been called "women troubadours of God."

It is impossible to give a comprehensive account of all the Beguines, especially as new material about different figures is constantly coming to light. Each woman is an individual, with her own history, and her own religious and mystical vocation. Yet what unites the Beguines is their intense love and longing for God. Out of the large number of Beguines in the Netherlands, Germany, and France, three different figures from the thirteenth and early fourteenth centuries are presented here. They are roughly contemporaries, although it is unlikely that they knew of each other's work. All three emphasize love above knowledge, and write in praise of an intensive love mysticism between the human soul and God.

St. Mechtild of Magdeburg (c. 1210-97)

Mechtild was born between 1207 and 1210 in Lower Saxony, in Germany. She came from a well-to-do family, probably of noble descent, and received a good education, as is evident from her literary style and knowledge of court manners. We know little of her family except that she had a younger brother. Early in her life, at the age of twelve, she received a revelation from the Holy Spirit, and at the age of twenty-three she moved to the city of Magdeburg to live there as a Beguine, joining other women in a community caring for the sick and needy.

For many years she concealed the exceptional graces bestowed on her, but finally she confided in her Dominican confessor who encouraged her to write down her experiences of loving union with God. Although Mechtild felt unworthy that "a poor despised little woman should write this book out of God's heart and mouth," she began the task which took her many years. She wrote on loose sheets of paper that were later collected, copied, and translated from Low German into Latin, and thus the first six parts of her book *The Flowing Light of the Godhead* were circulated during her lifetime. It is possible that Dante may have read them, for there are parts of his *Divine Comedy* which are strikingly similar to certain scenes in Mechtild's work.

Sunshine in the Beguinage, by Norman Garstin (1847-1926). The tradition of the Beguines continued in the Low Countries into the modern period, and several beguinages can still be seen today in Belgium and the Netherlands. (Crawford Municipal Art Gallery, Cork, Ireland)

Contemporary readers were surprised "at the masculine way in which this book is written," and Mechtild felt aggrieved about this, for she attributed the strength of her writing about the power of divine love to the same God who made the apostles strong and fearless, gave Moses courage before the Pharaoh, and Daniel wisdom to speak as a youth.

Yet her work seems to have attracted considerable clerical antagonism. After having been a Beguine in Magdeburg for about forty years, it is thought that in order to escape persecution and calumny in her old age, she joined the Cistercian convent of Helfta, a remarkable center of learning, where the abbess Gertrude of Hackeborn received her in 1270. It is here that Mechtild wrote the seventh and last part of her book.

She recorded her visions and spiritual union through the language of courtly love, expressed in the form of dialogues between Mechtild and Christ. *The Flowing Light of the Godhead* consists of a series of long and short poems, interspersed with narrative prose. The dialogues take different forms: they are between God and the Soul, between Lady Soul and Lady Love and other allegorical figures such as Fidelity, Constancy, Pain, and Withdrawal of God. The major theme of the book is a celebration of God's love. The soul is created for loving communion with God, as a bride with her bridegroom, in a relationship of total mutuality.

Mechtild's work is motivated by the deep desire that the soul return to its original being in God. It is her true nature to live in the flowing light of the Godhead, just as it is a bird's nature to fly in the air and a fish's nature to swim in water. She has emanated from the heart of God where she must return, but she discovers her utter nakedness before and in God: "Lord, now I am a naked soul!" Yet her intense love pours out in praise of God:

> *O God! so generous in the outpouring*
> *of Thy gifts!*
> *So flowing in Thy Love!*
> *So burning in Thy desire!*
> *So fervent in union!*
> *O Thou who doest rest on my heart*
> *Without whom I could no longer live!*

These love poems between God and the soul may be influenced by Bernard of Clairvaux's sermons on the Song of Songs, with which Mechtild was probably familiar, as she was with the works of Richard of St. Victor and Joachim of Fiore. Her poems use the cadences of worldly love songs and the conventions of courtly love poetry as well as the rich symbolism of biblical imagery.

Written as it was, over twenty or even thirty years, one can glimpse from *The Flowing Light of the Godhead* how the stages of Mechtild's spiritual journey corresponded to those of her physical and emotional life. The last part of the book, written in old age, makes her reflect on her childhood and youth. But she also speaks of her illnesses and laments the decline of her physical strength. Yet God assures her: "Thy childhood was a companion of My Holy Spirit; thy youth was a bride of My humanity, in thine old age thou art a humble house-wife of My Godhead." Thus she could maintain her confidence and trust in God's love and ever present help, knowing full well that she was never alone.

Many passages in Mechtild's book offer comfort and consolation to seeking souls at all stages of life. She writes vividly about the world of corruption and suffering from which she wishes to see Christianity delivered. But she has little to say about the persecution of the Jews which took place in medieval Germany and which she must have known about at Magdeburg. It was probably from St. Bernard and Richard of St. Victor that Mechtild learnt the great Neoplatonic and patristic theme of the return to our original nature in God. She also uses the ancient image of "living in the desert" in a metaphorical way, as in the following poem, "The Desert Has Twelve Things," which makes skilled use of paradox to a striking effect:

> *You must love no-thingness,*
> *You must flee something,*
> *You must remain alone*
> *And go to nobody.*
> *You must be very active*
> *And free of all things.*
> *You must deliver the captives*
> *And force those who are free.*
> *You must comfort the sick*
> *And yet have nothing yourself.*
> *You must drink the water of suffering*
> *And light the fire of Love with the*
> *   wood of the virtues.*
> *Thus you live in the true desert.*

Mechtild's book *The Flowing Light of the Godhead* was not preserved in its original Low German form, but has only come down to us in Middle High German and Latin translations. The German translation was only discovered in 1860 and has attracted considerable interest since then, especially in recent years. In some ways Mechtild of Magdeburg already points to a change in medieval thought and the beginnings of modern spirituality.

Hadewijch of Brabant (thirteenth century)

It is difficult to discover precise details about this Flemish female mystic who has left us a considerable body of writings, composed of *Poems, Visions,* and *Letters,* but we do not have a written account of Hadewijch's life. She is considered one of the creators of Dutch lyrical poetry, and it is thought that her works were written sometime during the second quarter of the thirteenth century. But they were forgotten after the fourteenth century. Medieval specialists rediscovered them only in the nineteenth century, and their first critical edition appeared in 1920. Thus it is not surprising that even today many books on Christian mystics do not mention Hadewijch.

It seems she was a Beguine, a "mistress" or spiritual guide to an unorganized group of Beguines to whom she speaks with authority. But some of her remarks also point to considerable difficulties and opposition to her from both inside and outside her own community. Like other Beguines, she seems to have devoted herself to charitable activity, such as the care of the sick.

Given Hadewijch's knowledge of Latin and French and her use of courtly imagery, it is thought that she came from a noble family, probably from somewhere around Antwerp or Brussels, for she writes in the dialect of medieval Brabant. Influenced by the love mysticism of Bernard of Clairvaux and others, her work represents an "experiential radicalization of the theology of love." Love is her spouse, her companion, her Lady Mistress, her God. Love is a person to whom one can speak, a lady, a queen whose strength and richness are praised. But love is above all Divine Love whose gifts inebriate and whose strength makes her experience all the rage and fury, the suffering of love when love becomes inaccessible. The contradictions and paradoxes are held in tension in her poems, as when she describes love as:

Sometimes burning and sometimes cold,
Sometimes timid and sometimes bold,
The whims of Love are manifold...
Sometimes gracious and sometimes cruel,
Sometimes far and sometimes near...
Sometimes light, sometimes heavy,
Sometimes sombre and sometimes bright,
In freeing consolation, in stifling anguish,
In taking and in giving,
Thus live the spirits
Who wander here below,
Along the paths of Love.

The storms and fury of love bring moments of despair as well as rapture and delight. This is expressed in her *Letters* written to others, giving them advice about the relationship between God and the soul. "The soul is a bottomless abyss in which God suffices to Himself and ever finds His plenitude in her, just as the soul ever does in Him. The soul is a free way for the passage of God from His profound depths; again, God is a way for the passage of the soul into her freedom, that is to say, into the abyss of the Divine Being, which can be touched only by the abyss of the soul." God is the illumination of the soul and once so illumined, the soul can follow God's will

Christ taking leave of his mother before the passion. A woodcut from Albrecht Dürer's book *The Life of the Virgin* (1504-5). Like Christian women today, medieval women mystics were inspired and affirmed by the Gospel story that the risen Christ first appeared to three women whom he assured of his continued presence and teachings. (British Museum, London)

in a perfect manner and do everything "in accordance with the truth of Love's laws."

In her later poems, Hadewijch uses striking language and metaphysical themes which were to be further developed by the German mystic Meister Eckhart. She speaks of nakedness and void, of the shedding of the will, of all images and forms in order to attain "pure and naked Nothingness" so that union with God is no longer experienced as the highest stage of beatitude but as a plunge into boundless unknowing, into the "wild desert" of the Divine Essence. To reach the divine summit nothing must remain to encumber the spirit: "The circle of things must shrink and be annihilated so that the circle of nakedness can grow and extend in order to embrace the All."

Hadewijch's language expresses the super-abundance of spiritual experience, reflecting her participation in the Trinitarian mysteries. She celebrates the divine names: Presence in the Son, Overflow in the Holy Spirit, Totality in the Father. Union with the three persons of the Holy Trinity in active and contemplative life leads to ultimate Unity, to the repose and silence of the soul in the depths of God. There exists an abyss between this experience of spiritual plenitude and her efforts to say something about it. Words are utterly insufficient here, yet they must be used to communicate something of the "blessedness of being lost in the fruition of Love" to those who are capable of receiving such a message.

The stark love mysticism of Hadewijch provided much inspiration to the fourteenth-century mystic, Jan van Ruusbroec, who knew her works. Like her, he emphasized the primacy of love, its storms and delights, as well as the idea of "living in the Trinity." But not all women mystics were revered and accepted; some suffered much opposition and even persecution, such as Marguerite Porete, who fell victim to the Inquisition and died at the stake for her views.

Marguerite Porete (d. 1310)

Few details are known about Marguerite, who does not seem to have been part of a community of Beguines, but lived by herself and wrote down her teachings in an appealing vernacular form, producing a book which became very popular. She taught a mysticism of pure love: God is love and love is God, which the soul, stripped of all else, can reach and be fused with. Her famous text *Mirror of Simple Souls* was rediscovered in 1867, although the link with its author was clearly established only as recently as 1946.

Marguerite was courageous, persevering in her teaching, as explained in her book, even when faced with the greatest difficulties and staunchest opposition from the Church authorities. Her work was condemned by the Bishop of Cambrai in 1306 and then publicly burned on the square of Valenciennes. Furthermore, its use was prohibited under pain of excommunication. Later, Marguerite was imprisoned in Paris for eighteen months. When she refused to retract her teaching, she was threatened with death, declared a relapsed heretic, and on June 1, 1310 she was burned at the stake on the Place de Grève in Paris in the presence of civil and ecclesiastical authorities. A large crowd of people was present too, but they rather took her side when witnessing Marguerite's attitude to death.

Although it is not entirely clear which detailed charges were brought against her, it is of considerable significance that the documents of Marguerite's trial were preserved so that historians can now work on them. It seems that Marguerite was put to death for her views which "render the soul simple" and make it free through the radical, unconditional love for God. This radical sense of freedom and what has been

Marguerite of Angouleme (Navarre), attributed to François Clouet (1522-72). She became a strong supporter of Marguerite Porete's ideas—her radical, unconditional love for God and her "mysticism of abandonment"—a hundred years after the latter's burning at the stake. Marguerite Porete's "heresy" was to preach the essential freedom of the soul. (Musée Condé, Chantilly, France)

called a "mysticism of self-abandonment" made her appear a threat to the institutional Church and its authority.

But Marguerite's death did not put an end to the popularity of the *Mirror of Simple Souls*, which enjoyed a great success in Europe during the fourteenth and fifteenth centuries, especially in women's convents. The Inquisition was unable to suppress the text in spite of continued persecutions. Written in Old French, the book has only recently been recognized as a major spiritual *oeuvre* of French literature, a work which was able to overcome linguistic barriers more than any other mystical text in the vernacular through being translated into Old Italian, Middle English, and even Latin.

Marguerite's work is presented in the form of a play with allegorical characters, the chief ones being Soul and Lady Love (who is God Himself in his essence). It stresses the "annihilation" of the soul, its nothingness before God. A hundred years after its condemnation the *Mirror of Simple Souls* found a famous supporter in the person of Marguerite of Navarre, the only sister of Francis I, who was friendly with the nuns at the Madeleine Convent of Orléans where the original version of the *Mirror*, in Old French, was kept. Later in her life, Marguerite of Navarre mentions in her own writing the *Mirror* as one of the books "which follow unconditionally the intention of the Sacred Bible." She says about Marguerite Porete, its author:

Oh, how attentive this woman was
to receive that love which burned
her own heart and those to which she spoke!
Well she knew by her subtle spirit
the true friend whom she named Noble.

Marguerite's work is not based on visions, like Hildegard's or Mechtild's, but it is presented as an inner dialog of the soul who after the practice of asceticism and her obedience to the commandments completely and utterly abandons herself to the will of God and has no more will of her own. Central is the theme of liberation, of abandonment and "annihilation" of the soul who stands in complete "nakedness" before God. Such "simple, annihilated souls" only "dwell in the will and desire of love" as the full title of her book proclaims. And God is this love that meets all desires and gives all joys. Abandoning herself, the soul has no more will and desire except that of God. She has lost her individual identity like a river that has emptied itself into the sea.

Marguerite praises those who love without question. Without denying the role of doctrines or the practice of virtues, she preaches the essential freedom of the soul, and it is this freedom which was a real threat to the authority of the learned and the power of established religious institutions. In 1311-12, the Council of Vienne condemned the teachings of her *Mirror*, together with others aspects of northern mysticism, so that eventually the movement of the Beguines declined in the Church. Yet these medieval women mystics broke free from established scholarly and literary conventions in praising the powers of the human heart and celebrating the love of God in the popular tongues of their time. They spoke with great spiritual authority to their contemporaries. Centuries have passed and much has changed since then, but the freshness and lyrical beauty of their works still speaks to us today, as do some of the values they lived and died for.

THE RHINELAND MYSTICS

Among all the medieval mystics, the Rhineland mystics are perhaps the best known today. They are widely accessible, and cited more frequently than any others. Their message has a directness and freshness of expression that communicates itself across the centuries. Initially one might expect that all mystics from the Rhine region would be counted as Rhineland mystics; and this would for example include Hildegard of Bingen, whose work we have already met. But the term "Rhineland mystics" is customarily used in a more restricted sense. It refers only to the mystics of the fourteenth century who lived in Germany and the Low Countries. It applies particularly to a group of several men—Meister Eckhart, Henry Suso, Johannes Tauler, and Jan van Ruusbroec.

The fourteenth century experienced a revival of interest in the apophatic mysticism of Denys, or Dionysius the Areopagite. The influence of his thought can be seen in both the Rhenish and the English mystics, although the former were more speculatively inclined than the latter. The Rhineland mystics combined the traditional Neoplatonic themes of contemplation with a spirit of analysis and reflection learnt from the medieval schoolmen. The most daring and original of the Rhenish mystics was Meister Eckhart whose disciples were Johannes Tauler and Henry Suso. These three Germans all belonged to the Dominican Order. Suso is seen as the most intimate and personal mystic; Tauler was known as an inspiring preacher, whereas the Flemish mystic Jan van Ruusbroec was probably the most profound.

These men, deeply involved in the theo-logical debates of their own age, describe the deepest levels of inward experience where God is known in the inner recesses of the human soul, a most intimate presence that is also a

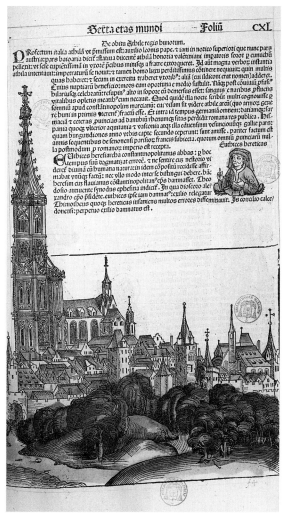

Strasburg Cathedral, detail of an engraving from the Nuremberg Chronicles, 1493. The city of Strasburg was an important religious center in medieval Europe. Meister Eckhart spent some time here and his ideas may have been influenced by several religious groups living in the city. (Bibliothèque Mazarine, Paris)

transcendence. Their message addresses us so directly because it relates to a search for what is most essential to religion, its deepest, most inward dimension, and it emphasizes a real indwelling of ourselves in God and of God in us. The mysticism of the Rhineland is known in German as "*Wesensmystik,*" a mysticism of being or essence, whereas the mysticism of the Beguines is called "*Liebesmystik,*" or love mysticism. Mysticism of being is concerned with the ultimate ground of all things, with God in Himself or the Godhead. Ideas central to this Rhenish mysticism are the ground of the soul, the path of self-stripping and the process of detachment, whereby the mystic advances to the knowledge of an imageless and formless God, a *Deus nudus.* Not all these ideas found easy acceptance; some, particularly the teachings of Meister Eckhart, were even condemned as heretical.

Meister Eckhart (1260-1327)

Born of a noble family in Hochheim, in the province of Thuringia in the eastern part of Germany, Eckhart entered the Dominican Order at a young age. He began his training in Erfurt, but soon moved on to the more advanced *studium generale* in Cologne. This enjoyed a particularly high reputation at that time because of its association with the teaching of Albertus Magnus and Thomas of Aquinas. Eckhart completed his studies in Paris where he became Master (or *Meister*) of Theology in 1302, and was henceforth

Detail from *The Entrance to Heaven*, by Hieronymus Bosch (c. 1450-1516). The "mysticism of being" of the Rhineland teaches that the mystic is drawn into an imageless and formless Godhead, a transcendent center that is the ultimate ground and fulfillment of all things. (Doges Palace, Venice)

known as "Meister Eckhart."

He soon rose to eminence in the hierarchy of the Dominican Order. In 1304 he was made provincial of the Saxon Province of his Order, and in 1307 he was entrusted with the reform of its houses in Bohemia. In 1311 he was sent as a teacher to Paris, but soon returned to Germany, living first in Strasburg and later in Cologne, where he became known as a great, popular preacher who enjoyed an immensely high status and reputation during his lifetime.

Strasburg was then one of the foremost religious centers in Germany, containing a wide spectrum of religious groups, including Beguines and Brethren of the Free Spirit, and Eckhart may well have been influenced by some of their ideas. It was in 1322 or earlier that he was sent to Cologne to take the place of Albertus Magnus at the *studium generale* where Eckhart could propound his ideas. These were expressed in many works, written in both German and Latin, and especially in his *Sermons* and *Treatises.*

Meister Eckhart was highly acclaimed as a teacher and thinker among his contemporaries. His teaching can be summed up as an attempt to express the highest mystical union in terms of a daring metaphysics, deeply rooted in the Augustinian theological tradition. In his mysticism, the ground of God and the ground of the soul are the same ground. His strong emphasis on the absorption of the self into God in the unitive mystical experience may well have been the source of his difficulties with the Church.

The Archbishop of Cologne at that time, a Franciscan, was much opposed to mystical speculation which he associated with heretical sects. Given his attitude, it is not surprising that in 1326 he began proceedings against Eckhart, who was tried before the episcopal court. The case dragged on, and Eckhart appealed to the Pope, though he acknowledged that many of his teachings had been misunderstood or distorted, but he did not consider himself a heretic. Unfortunately Eckhart died before a final judgment was made. In March 1329 the Pope published a bull, condemning twenty-six articles from Eckhart's Latin and two from his German works.

This meant that from now on Meister Eckhart's teachings were met with suspicion, that his works fell into obscurity and many were lost. A modern revival of interest occurred when an Austrian scholar published a selection of Eckhart's German works in 1855. This led to a rediscovery of this great German mystical writer by the Romantic poets. It also produced a great many divergent interpretations, claiming Meister Eckhart as a forerunner of Luther's emphasis on faith or of Hegel's pantheism, or of other philosophical views. In recent years, more careful historical scholarship and detailed studies have led to a much better knowledge and revised assessment of his work so that in 1980 the Dominican Order could formally request that all censures on his teachings be lifted.

Steeped in Neoplatonism, Meister Eckhart's teachings are at one level deeply dualistic while ultimately celebrating the highest unity. To find such unity, we must retreat from the world and its images to an inner state of utter denudedness in order to experience the "birth of God in the soul." Eckhart was preoccupied with God as Being. He drew the famous distinction between *God* and the *Godhead*. God is revealed to us as a person, but behind this revelation, this manifestation, there is the unrevealed Godhead, the "ground" of God, undifferentiated and above all distinction, an eternal unity of which nothing can be said, the "Nameless Nothing", the unoriginated purity of Being, the *puritas essendi,* the Eternal Now which we can meet only in utter stillness and silence, and which Eckhart celebrates in soaring thoughts and startling paradoxes. Meister Eckhart's metaphysics of the Godhead is sometimes compared with what Indian Vedanta teaches about *Brahman* without attributes, especially as found in the works of Shankara.

For Meister Eckhart, human union with God is made possible through the divine spark in the soul, the *Seelenfünklein*, both the center and the ground of the soul, partaking of the very nature of God. He speaks of this spark also as "the citadel in the soul" or the "light" of the soul. But in order to be united with God, the soul must be purified by practicing asceticism, detachment, silence, and withdrawal, by forgetting ideas and concepts, and by not loving anything that is created. Human perfection consists in becoming "distant from creatures and free from them, to respond in the same way to all things, not to be broken by adversity nor carried away by prosperity, not to rejoice more in one thing than in another, not to be frightened or grieved by one thing more than another."

The soul's union with God is immeasurably deep and is the soul's greatest desire. Through such union the soul becomes through grace what God is like by nature. The soul then knows God

Illumination from a French Book of Hours showing the different monastic orders, fifteenth century. The mystical teachings of the Christian Church were mainly transmitted through the religious orders. (Bibliothèque Nationale, Paris)

as God is in Godself. In one of his sermons Eckhart writes: "The union of God with the soul is so great that it is scarcely to be believed. And God is in himself so far above that no form of knowledge or desire can ever reach him.... Desire is deep, immeasurably so. But nothing that the intellect can grasp and nothing that desire can desire is God. Where understanding and desire end, there is darkness and there God's radiance begins."

Eckhart also speaks of *jubilatio*, of the joy of those who know God. His high, abstract system of thought seems to shun practical devotions, yet many eloquent and vivid passages speak about everyday concerns, instructing his listeners and readers to find the peace of God and be with God always and everywhere. Here is a passage from Meister Eckhart's *Talks of Instruction*:

> *Whoever has God truly as a companion, is with him in all places, both on the street and among people, as well as in church or in the desert or in a monastic cell....Why is this so? It is so because such a person possesses God alone, keeping their gaze fixed upon God, and thus all things become God for him or her. Such people bear God in all their deeds and in all the places they go, and it is God alone who is the author of all their deeds.... If we keep our eyes fixed on God alone, then truly he must work in us, and nothing, neither the crowd nor any place, can hinder him in this. And so nothing will be able to hinder us, if we desire and seek God alone, and take pleasure in nothing else.*

Henry Suso (1295-1366)

Another Dominican mystic of this period is the Blessed Henry Suso, or Heinrich Seuse, to give him his original German name. Son of a noble Swabian family, he was born near Lake Constance, on the border between Switzerland and Germany. His father was very worldly, his mother deeply devout. As he tells us in his own *Life*, written in later years, one of his earliest memorable experiences occurred on the death of his mother when he was still young. She appeared in a vision and told him to love God, then kissed and blessed him, and disappeared. Suso's sense of loneliness and abandonment, his excessive asceticism in later life, harshly maltreating his body in imitation of Christ's suffering, and his expressions of tender love addressed to God may all have been linked to "starved human affections seeking an outlet," as Evelyn Underhill suggested.

Suso entered the Dominican Order at the age of thirteen, but found monastic life difficult until he experienced a conversion and spiritual awakening. He subsequently studied under Eckhart in Cologne, and became a devoted follower and great admirer of his beloved teacher. By 1326 Suso was back in Constance, where he wrote his famous *Büchlein der Wahrheit*, or *Little Book of Truth*, which is full of mystical reflection. Originally written to combat the Brethren of the Free Spirit, who consisted of various mystical sects professing to be independent from ecclesiastical authority and thus deemed to be heretical, this book of practical meditations became one of the classics of German mysticism.

The *Little Book of Truth* finishes with a hundred brief meditations on Christ's passion, for it is Christ's humanity that is the way to know God. Suso's book was widely read in the fourteenth and fifteenth centuries, and included Thomas à

Illumination from *The Exemplar,* by Henry Suso, on the theme of compassion.
(Bibliothèque Nationale et Universitaire, Strasburg)

Kempis among its admirers. During 1334 Suso himself made a Latin adaptation of this work, but he also produced several other writings, notably the *Little Book of Eternal Wisdom*.

Suso preached widely in the Upper Rhineland and Switzerland, enjoying great popularity wherever he went. Yet his defense of Eckhart brought some rebuke from his Order and led to his being deprived of his teaching position. He was greatly valued as a spiritual director in many women's convents, especially those of the Dominican Order. The savage asceticism and austerities which he practiced over many years are vividly described in his *Life*, where he speaks of himself in the third person: "In winter he suffered very much from the frost…His feet were full of sores, his legs dropsical, his knees bloody and seared, his loins covered with scars from the horsehair, his body wasted, his mouth parched with intense thirst, his hands tremulous from weakness. Amid these torments he spent his nights and days; and he endured them all out of the greatness of the love which he bore in his heart to the Divine and Eternal Wisdom, our Lord Jesus Christ, whose agonizing sufferings he ought to imitate."

But after some twenty years of severe ascetic practices, he abandoned them as nothing more than a beginning on the way to the highest knowledge of God, whose overwhelming beauty he praised with great tenderness: "Ah, gentle God, if Thou art so lovely in Thy creatures, how exceedingly beautiful and ravishing Thou must be in Thyself!…Praise and honor be to the unfathomable immensity that is in Thee!"

Suso must have left a deep impression on his contemporaries, for the veneration of the "Blessed Henry Suso" began soon after his death, although officially the Church did not beatify him until 1831.

Johannes Tauler (c. 1300-61)

If Meister Eckhart's teachings are highly abstract, intellectual and speculative, Tauler's, being much closer to ordinary Christian life and its devotions, are easier to absorb and follow, although he retains much of Eckhart's thought and terminology and shows a genuine understanding of his message.

Tauler, like Eckhart, entered the Dominican Order at a young age in Strasburg, where he probably came under Eckhart's influence and also that of Henry Suso. He would have received a basic education in the arts and in theology, but he was not singled out for advanced studies. Thus he was not sent to the *studium generale,* as Eckhart had been, and received much less formal training. Tauler never wrote in Latin, the universal language of medieval scholars. While he possessed a healthy suspicion of mere book learning, he nevertheless had a deep grasp of theological truths and, in about 1325, was ordained a Dominican priest.

He soon became famous as a spiritual director, especially of nuns, and acquired a tremendous reputation as a popular preacher. His popularity probably also had much to do with his many travels. He even visited Groenendael, outside Brussels, to meet Jan van Ruusbroec. During the Black Death of 1348, he devoted himself to the care of the sick, which further increased his popularity and reputation.

The years 1338-43 were spent in the city of Basle where he had close contact with a group of *Gottesfreunde* or Friends of God, a widespread, loosely grouped movement which emphasized mystical, visionary, and prophetic experience over mere head and book knowledge. Devoted to ascetic practices and renunciation, these small groups of Friends, guided by a leader, denounced the abuses of the Church and considered themselves as an inner Church directed by the Holy Spirit. They based their teaching on Eckhart's notion of the divine spark and had a considerable following without being against the Church as such.

Tauler is so closely associated with Strasburg, where he died and is buried, that he is sometimes called "Johannes Tauler of Strasburg." His popularity meant that numerous works were later attributed to him, but few are genuine. He left eighty-four sermons in German, recorded by his listeners, most likely written down by nuns. But the clarity and form of these texts makes one think that he revised or at least approved their final version. These *Sermons* were first printed in 1498 and then translated into Latin in 1548. They found their widest diffusion in this Latin form and became known as far away as Spain. Luther read Tauler's German *Sermons* and greatly admired "such sterling theology, equal to that of the ancients." But this referred mainly to Tauler's spiritual advice on practical matters, whereas Luther mistrusted his essentially mystical teaching.

Like Eckhart, Tauler emphasized the indwelling of God in the human soul without stressing the identity of creature and creator to the same degree. Tauler has more room for the role of grace and for the place of the Holy Spirit in mystical union. His deeply mystical theology is, however, like Eckhart's, based on "the uncreated ground of the soul" present in all human beings, the soul's insatiable hunger for God, and the need for passivity so that God can work in the soul. Yet the experience of this work can be a form of suffering, a teaching whereby he already anticipates the later "dark night of the soul" in St. John of the Cross.

Tauler also stresses the immense spiritual value of our everyday tribulations. He describes the mystic way as consisting in the practice of virtues, especially that of humility and abandonment to the will of God. The desired union with God produces in the soul greater love and charity as well as strength to lead a life of suffering and self-sacrifice. The difference between Meister Eckhart and Johannes Tauler was later summarized by contrasting Eckhart as a *Lehrmeister,* a "master of thinking," with Tauler as a *Lebemeister* or a "master of living."

Yet Tauler follows Eckhart in describing God in negative terms when he writes:

> God is pure Being, a waste of calm seclusion....much nearer than anything is to itself in the depth of the heart, but He is hidden from all our senses. He is far above every outward thing and every thought, and is found only where thou hidest thyself in the secret place of thy heart, in the quiet solitude where no word is spoken, where is neither creature nor image nor fancy. This is the quiet Desert of the Godhead, the Divine Darkness—dark from His own surpassing brightness, as the shining of the sun is darkness to weak eyes, for in the presence of its brightness our eyes are like the eyes of the swallow in the bright sunlight.

The way to God is for Tauler the *via negativa* of the Desert Fathers and of Dionysius, finding God in withdrawal and the wilderness. At the same time he also possesses a strongly affirmative spirituality, as when he says that works of love are more acceptable to God than even contemplation, that spiritual enjoyment is food for the soul which should be taken only to support us in our active work. Thus his mystical teaching is eminently practical, translating experience into action. The down-to-earth, common-sense humility of this Dominican mystic is well expressed in his often quoted words: "One man can spin, another can make shoes, and all these are gifts of the Holy Spirit. I tell you, if I were not a priest, I should esteem it a great gift that I was able to make shoes, and I would try to make them so well as to be a pattern to all."

Jan van Ruusbroec (1293-1381)

Another celebrated Rhenish mystic, the Flemish priest Jan van Ruusbroec was a friend of both Tauler and Suso, and much inspired by the Beguine Hadewijch and the Cistercian nun Beatrijs of Nazareth (1220-68). He shares with these two women the mystical themes of the primacy of love and the idea of "living in the Trinity." This Trinitarian love mysticism, actualized in the world through grace, has distant origins in St. Augustine and shows the influence of Bernard of Clairvaux and other writers.

Ruusbroec was a figure of luminous sanctity, who was gifted with great literary expression. This is evident from his great works *The Sparkling Stone* and *The Spiritual Espousals,* sometimes called *The Adornment of the Spiritual Marriage.*

Born in 1293 in Ruusbroec, near Brussels, he came from a simple village background. He moved to Brussels at the age of nine to live in the house of his uncle, a canon at the collegial church of St. Gudule, now the cathedral of Brussels. He undertook his studies at the chapter school of St. Gudule and became a priest in 1317, serving on the church staff for many years. But dissatisfied with the low spiritual standards in the city, he withdrew in 1343 with his uncle and some other priests to a hermitage in Groenendael ("Green Dale") in the forest of Soignes, south-east of Brussels, where the men could live a more secluded, contemplative life. It is here that Ruusbroec wrote many of his works.

This group of men was soon joined by others. In 1349 they adopted the rules of Augustinian Canons and Ruusbroec became their prior, an office he held until his death. It was not long before Groenendael became a celebrated center of pilgrimage visited by Johannes Tauler and Geert de Groote, Ruusbroec's most famous disciple. Groenendael exerted a lasting influence through the popular movement of spiritual reform founded by de Groote and known as Brethren of the Common Life, or New Devotion (*devotio moderna*). This movement affected both Erasmus and Luther, and produced its most celebrated adherent in Thomas à Kempis and his widely read *Imitation of Christ.*

Ruusbroec's lack of university education has sometimes been unnecessarily emphasized. He was certainly no illiterate rural mystic, although he always maintained that his writing was directly impelled by the Holy Spirit. But as a priest he would have known Latin, and he read the works of other mystics. He was also deeply

The face of God covered by a whirling sun. This is the dazzling darkness of divine effacement. The Rhineland mystics describe the essence of the Godhead as being without form, a divine, luminous darkness. "Where understanding and desire end, there is darkness and there God's radiance begins." Rothschild Canticles. (Beinecke Library, Yale University Library, New Haven, Ct.)

steeped in vernacular mystical literature, for example the writings of Hadewijch.

Ruusbroec left eleven spiritual treatises. Though based on scriptural exegesis, they are all concerned with the soul's absorption into the inner life of the Trinity through love. During his own time his writings exercised much less influence on his contemporaries than his saintly life; although some of his ideas did circulate in England during the fourteenth century, chiefly in the Carthusian Order. It was, above all, the sixteenth-century Latin translation of his works by a Carthusian monk from Cologne which made the Flemish mystic known all over Europe.

Ruusbroec's famous and most systematic work is *The Spiritual Espousals*, probably written in about 1346, although some of his shorter works, such as *The Book of Supreme Truth*, or *The Sparkling Stone*, are perhaps more accessible. According to Evelyn Underhill, the latter work in particular reaches "the high water mark of mystical literature." The book takes its title from Revelation 2:17: "To him who is victorious I will give a sparkling stone, and on the stone will be written

The Trinity, woven within a circle of cloth. Ruusbroec was one of the great exponents of Trinitarian love mysticism, which stressed the loving inner unity and community of the divine being. The cloth is an allusion to the curtain of the Tabernacle. Rothschild Canticles. (Beinecke Library, Yale University Library, New Haven, Ct.)

a new name, known to none but him that receives it." For Ruusbroec, the sparkling stone is a symbol of mystical union, and also of Christ's humanity. The stone is white and shining, radiating the glory of God, a flawless mirror in which all things are alive. Its roundness signifies that truth has no beginning or end; its smoothness means that truth is equitable; its slightness shows that although truth is immaterial, it bears upon heaven and earth by its strength.

The Sparkling Stone says less about the stone itself than about what a human being must do to be worthy of receiving it. For this reason it also bears a second title: *The Treatise of Perfection of the Sons of God*. The three stages to perfection are traditionally called those of the beginner, the proficient, and the perfect.

In *The Sparkling Stone* Ruusbroec describes the three stages as those of the faithful servant, the secret friend, and the hidden son or "God-seeing man." From the outward, active life, marked by virtue and good works, the seeker progresses to the inner life, concerned with inward devotions, the life of grace, and movements of love towards God. At the highest, contemplative stage a "God-seeing life" is reached where the human being is drawn up through love into the inner flux and rhythms of the Trinity itself and loses itself in the abyss of God's love: "There we shall flow forth and flow out of ourselves into the uncomprehended abundance of God's riches and goodness. There we will melt and be dissolved, eternally taken up in the maelstrom of God's glory."

Ruusbroec's mystical doctrine has its source in the teaching that human beings are made in the image of God and thus possess the potential for deification. All his thought is permeated by the image of the Trinity. There is first of all a simple Trinity in God, consisting of God's essence or Godhead, the divine nature, and the three persons, Father, Son and Holy Spirit. Within the human being, created in this image, there exists a threefold "created trinity," consisting of spirit, reason, and the essential nature of the soul. Then there are the three stages of the spiritual ladder—the active, interior and contemplative life—by which the created spirit can ascend to God.

"I am he who does not move, but moves all things." According to Ruusbroec, the world is aflame with God's loving presence, which draws the soul into a "fury of love." The symbolism of this image links the triune creator god with the wheels of Ezekiel's vision. Rothschild Canticles. (Beinecke Library, Yale University Library, New Haven, Ct.)

Through turning inward, the heart must be freed of all images. Sinking into an "imageless nudity," inward freedom is achieved, through which union with God can be found, a life of secret or inward friendship wherein the "true sons and daughters of God" are rapt out of themselves and "burned up in the flame of love." This highest union is attained only by a few, and remains momentary in the present life. After losing or finding oneself in an immeasurable abyss above reason, melted into union, light and truth, the vision ends and the human being "falls back into reason" and the ordinariness of daily life. In seeing God, the soul becomes God without ever losing its own identity.

It is an active, affirmative vision of love, for the power of this seeing and knowing of God must empower those "who live in the spirit" to share the blessings they have received and to spend themselves on those who are in need. Reaching the transcendent God is thus not a passing from one life to another, but a perpetual deepening, heightening and enriching of human existence and common life.

Christ as the Fount of Life. In an image taken from the Song of
Songs, he is enthroned on a grassy mountain, with a fountain at
his feet. He raises his right hand in blessing. The three streams of
living water refer to the Trinity. Rothschild Canticles. (Beinecke
Library, Yale University Library, New Haven, Ct.)

In this illumination, Christ enfolds the Spiritual Bride in a loving embrace. The image is full of symbolic references to the Song of Songs. The changing seasons in the landscape below reflect the transformation and renewal of the soul. Rothschild Canticles. (Beinecke Library, Yale University Library, New Haven, Ct.)

Ruusbroec speaks of the union with God in passionate terms. Learning of God's love, the soul experiences a "gaping and inner craving," a stir and storm of fury with a heat so great that love flashes between the soul and God like lightning in the sky. This fury of love cannot be appeased, but "from each mutual renewing touch come yet more storms of love." The soul thirsts and hungers for God,

...for ever striving for what it lacks, ever swimming against the stream. One cannot leave it, one cannot have it: one cannot lack it, one cannot gain it: one cannot tell it, one cannot conceal it, for it is above reason and under-standing....But if we look deep within ourselves, there we shall feel God's Spirit driving and urging us on in the impatience of love; and if we look high above ourselves, there we shall feel God's Spirit drawing us out of ourselves and bringing us to nothing in the essence of God, that is, in the essential love in which we are one with Him, the love which we possess deeper and wider than every other thing.

Ruusbroec's descriptions of mystical union have been greatly admired and have attracted many to study his works. The symbolist poet Maurice Maeterlinck translated *The Spiritual Espousals;* the philosopher Walter Stace edited some of Ruusbroec's works comparing his thoughts with those of the Indian Upanishads; Evelyn Underhill edited and extensively commented on his work in a book wholly devoted to Ruusbroec, whom she declared her favorite of all mystics.

The ideas of the fourteenth-century Rhineland mystics were made widely known during the fifteenth century through two popular works whose authors are unknown to us. The first, *German Theology,* or *Theologia Germanica,* one of the classic books of Western mystical literature, may be the work of a knight of the Teutonic Order, simply referred to as "the man from Frankfurt." Here we find a selective treatment of the great themes of Eckhart and Tauler, but with a special emphasis on the submission of the human will to the divine will, and a stress on a deeply felt, inward religion, and a certain resistance to the authority of the Church. The work sums up the spiritual teaching of the Friends of God movement and became immensely popular, influencing the first generation of Protestant reformers. Its message appealed greatly to the young Luther, who later said that with the exception of the Bible and Augustine's works, he had learned more about God, Christ, and the human condition from this book than any other.

A simple, undogmatic faith, with a passive acceptance of suffering and a special devotion to the Passion of Christ, is also the mark of the second of these two popular works, the *Book of Spiritual Poverty,* which emphasizes the need to combine external, freely chosen poverty with the internal poverty of detachment

During the next few centuries, the powerful insights and daring speculations of the Rhineland mystics were shaped into the pattern of a tradition which lived on almost more through these two devotional works than through the original writings of the mystics themselves. The two books shaped much of Christian piety and devotion, but in a less dynamic and original way than what had been expressed in the keen, soaring thought, the passionate feelings, and joyful celebrations of divine glory and splendor of the great theologian mystics of the Rhineland who preceded them.

ENGLISH MYSTICS

During the fourteenth and fifteenth centuries, the English Church experienced the rise of several outstanding mystics whose works possess an intimate, even homely flavor in their descriptions of the mystical life. In speaking about contemplation and union with God they use a language—mostly their native English tongue—marked by both affirmation and negation when describing the depth of divine life and unitive mystical experience. A considerable number of English medieval mystics have been rediscovered, and the manuscripts of yet more mystical authors may still be found in ancient libraries not ravaged by the Reformation. But the most outstanding, best-known figures are four mystics, sometimes grouped together as "Middle English" mystics because of the language in which they wrote. These four are the anonymous author of *The Cloud of Unknowing*, Richard Rolle, Walter Hilton, and Mother Julian.

Illumination from the *Chroniques de France et d'Angleterre* (c.1460) showing, on the left, the execution of Wat Tyler, leader of the Peasants' Revolt, in front of Richard II. On the right Richard addresses the rebels. The medieval English mystics lived in an age of great turmoil, and experienced their visions against the backdrop of the struggles and hardships of their times. (British Library, London)

The Cherub, from the De Lisle Psalter, English, fourteenth century. This mystical figure, echoing Ezekiel's vision, encompasses the six acts of morality and the thirty increments of virtue on its wings. It stands on a seven-spoked wheel inscribed with the seven works of mercy. (British Library, London)

There has been much debate about the influence of Continental mysticism on the English mystics. How far, for example, did the greatest German mystic, Meister Eckhart, influence English mysticism? Does *The Cloud of Unknowing* perhaps reflect some of the characteristic traits of the Dominican mystics of the Rhineland discussed earlier? It is difficult to give a definite answer to these questions. But it is probably much more likely that the Rhenish and English mystics share certain features because they were both influenced by Pseudo-Dionysius.

All four mystics belong to the fourteenth century. But the English mystics do not form a distinct school in the way that the Rhenish or later Spanish mystics do. They are too individual for that. They all wrote independently from each other, each with their own distinct style, although they knew something of each other's work.

They wrote at a restless time, full of conflict, when England was experiencing the debilitating repercussions of the Hundred Years' War. Also, during the middle of the century, in 1348-9 and again in 1361, England was ravaged by the plague which reduced the population by a third or even by as much as half. It was a time of major social change, and also of lawlessness. In 1381, the threatening Peasants' Revolt was put down, but none of this turmoil is reflected in the works of these four mystical writers. Yet it is perhaps not surprising that they wrote as solitaries, turning away from the chaos of their time to contemplate the unchanging holiness, great beauty, and all-consuming love of God.

The author of the *Cloud* wrote for another hermit; Rolle was himself a hermit; Hilton wrote for an anchoress; and Julian lived as anchoress, enclosed in her cell at Norwich. Other characteristics common to them is their writing in English—although Rolle and Hilton also wrote certain of their works in Latin—a strong personal testimony about their own religious experiences, and the accessibility of their writings, which share a directness and purpose based on common sense rather than artful rhetoric. Furthermore, they have in common the fundamentally affective nature of their mysticism and a shared distaste for theological learning. This affectivity is so strong in Rolle that the experience of God is described in terms of a spiritual sense of perception when he writes of eating and tasting God, feeling and touching, hearing and speaking, seeing and having God. Even Hilton, who is regarded as the theologian among the four, writes with great warmth and out of a personal rather than an abstract theological perspective.

The Cloud of Unknowing

Strongest in the Dionysian tradition of apophatic mysticism is this anonymous work, whose author, it has been suggested, could easily have been a woman but was more probably a priest, perhaps even a monk or hermit. His work is addressed to those following a life of solitude and contemplative prayer, concentrated on God alone and linked to a "mysticism of darkness," for ultimately God is beyond all description. If the mystic wishes to reach him, he must pass through the *cloud of forgetting* and pierce the *cloud of unknowing* that exists between himself and God.

The Cloud has a profound sense of the greatness of God, as is beautifully expressed in the following passage:

For silence is not God, nor speaking; fasting is not God, nor eating; solitude is not God, nor company; nor any other pair of opposites. He is hidden between them, and cannot be found by anything your soul does, but only by the love of your heart. He cannot be known by reason, he cannot be thought, caught, or sought by understanding. But he can be loved and chosen by the true, loving will of your heart.

The Cloud of Unknowing is a practical, unemotional book of instruction to the contemplative life, the first so written in the vernacular. It is stark in its radical insistence on stripping away all earthly ways of knowing. Other contemplatives of the time—Richard Rolle, Walter Hilton, Julian of Norwich—used more affirmative images, closer to ordinary daily experience, in expressing their understanding of contemplation which, in its fullest sense, meant the highest union with God. Such contemplation far transcended ordinary prayer and culminated in the direct, mystical knowledge of God. Such union, however, cannot be found by the soul alone—it is ultimately the gift of God's grace poured out on human beings in quest of the Divine.

Drawing on biblical stories, the mystical writers contrasted contemplation and action by comparing them to the parable of Martha and Mary in the New Testament. Martha, the woman busy around the house, symbolizes active involvement in the world whereas Mary, sitting quietly at Jesus's feet and listening to his words, exemplifies detachment and the quest for the contemplative life.

The mystical themes of contemplation and action, of divine knowledge and ultimate union with God, unfold in the lives of the fourteenth-century English mystics whose motive for writing was the attainment of contemplation, understood in the sense of the highest union with God, as it had been since the early Christian centuries.

Richard Rolle (c. 1300-41)

The earliest of the fourteenth-century English mystics, Richard Rolle, was born in Thornton-le-Dale in Yorkshire. Judging by the number of manuscripts we still possess of his writings, he was probably the most prolific and popular of the English mystics. But while his works are well known, the facts of his life are less certain. He seems to have studied in Oxford but broke off his studies at the age of nineteen, taking on a hermit's dress and way of life. He first lived on a

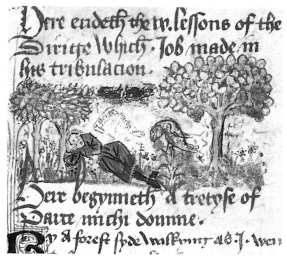

Early fifteenth-century miniature of the poet lying in a field and listening to a bird. From *A tretyse of parce michi Domine* by Richard Rolle, the father of English mysticism. His beautifully illustrated lyric poems and mystical works were widely circulated. (Bodleian Library, Oxford)

An illumination of Richard Rolle and another hermit from a manuscript collection of his works, c.1400. (Bodleian Library, Oxford)

friend's estate and later at various other places where he prayed, wrote, and gave guidance to others. His last years were spent attached to a Cistercian community at Hampole, near Doncaster. According to tradition, he probably died through helping others during the plague.

Rolle is sometimes called "the father of English mysticism." Best known among his numerous writings in English and Latin are his lyric poems, his commentary on the Psalms, his letters, the Latin treatise *Incendium Amori,* later translated into English as *The Fire of Love,* and *Ego Dormio,* or *I Sleep and My Heart Wakes,* based on a quotation from the biblical Song of Songs.

His great theme is the loving contemplation of God, linked to a passionate devotion to Christ and the holy name of Jesus on which one should ponder day and night. This is not unlike the Eastern Orthodox practice of the "Jesus prayer" with its continued repetition of the biblical sentence "Lord Jesus Christ, Son of God, have mercy upon me, a sinner." Far removed from the Pseudo-Dionysian tradition and Eckhart, Rolle's mysticism is firmly rooted in the humanity of Christ. His writings contain a clear testimony to the power of his own mystical experience and he also emphasizes the physical concomitants of this experience. His most distinctive terms for these are heat or fire, song, and sweetness.

Richard describes in *The Fire of Love* how, when sitting quietly meditating in the chapel, he suddenly had an intensive experience of heat and burning that was so real "as if it were being done by physical fire," just as "when a finger is placed in the fire." It was as if an elemental fire burned in the soul and set it aflame with a burning desire for the love of Christ, for God the beloved. The highest rapture into God is described using an imagery which is pervasively sexual, substantiated by biblical quotations and allusions. Such love scorns all pleasures of the flesh, all worldly concerns, all earthly rank, all "ostentation of glory and learning," but lives in strict poverty "in the love of God" by praying and meditating.

He praises the love of God to the exclusion of all else, he urges it even to the point of nagging and irritation. Theological knowledge is chastized and scorned, for God cannot be studied; God's vastness, mystery, and ineffability must be experienced. Vainglory, pride of self, and confusion are human presumptions which cannot reach God, nor is the human mind an adequate instrument for the discovery of the infinite spirit and theology is certainly not the path by which to discover the love of God.

His criticisms are not only directed against theologians "ensnared in infinite questionings" and the worldly wise, but even more strongly against women. Misogyny is found throughout his work. Rolle considers the love of women on earth as the chief rival to the love of God. While he admits that friendship with women is possible, he considers it hazardous and best to be avoided, for there is no sin more damnable than lust and no creature more dangerous to spiritual attainment than woman. This strongly anti-feminist streak mars Rolle's work for contemporary women. His approach to spirituality can also appear rather negative and dualistic to us today, as when he writes: "It is a perfect spiritual life to despise the world and to desire the joy of heaven; to destroy through the grace of God all the wicked desires of the flesh; to forget the solace and the love of your family, and only to love God." However exalted this love of God may be in Rolle, it seems to demand a high price, and one which sounds rather inhuman.

To follow his description of the stages of love and union, after the first stage of heat and burning, the stage of fire, there is the second stage of great joy in spirit brought about by heavenly song and intoxication, followed by a third stage of great sweetness which he compares to divine drunkenness. Thus he describes three stages of spiritual intensification, of rapture and ecstasy. In rapture there is not only the "rapture out of the senses," but also the rapture of the mind into God when the human spirit is lifted up to God in contemplation. The human being then sees "the door of heaven swing back to reveal the face of the Beloved," and his inner eye can "contemplate the things that are above."

Walter Hilton (1340-96)

What little we know about Hilton is derived from occasional manuscript references. From these it can be deduced that he studied at Cambridge, possibly canon law, and may have taken a degree. References to him as "Magister" may even indicate that he was a Doctor of Theology. He is certainly the most theological writer of the English mystics, but he lived as a hermit until, some time after 1375, he became an Augustinian canon at Thurgarton Priory, in Nottinghamshire, where he died in 1396.

Frontispiece to the 1525 edition of Walter Hilton's *Scala Perfctionis*. (British Library, London)

Illumination from *Scivias*, by Hildegard of Bingen, mid-twelfth century. The heavenly Jerusalem, or the ultimate goal of the human being, was depicted either as a real city or, in the abstract visionary manner of Hildegard, as a cosmic circle of perfection. (Abbey of St. Hildegard, Bingen, Germany)

He wrote profusely in English and Latin, but his fame rests almost entirely on his work *The Ladder* (or *Scale*) *of Perfection,* a masterpiece of spiritual writing which influenced numerous spiritual writers after Hilton. Written in English, it was first published in 1494, but is also known under its Latin title, *Scala Perfectionis.*

The *Ladder* falls into two parts. It is written for the spiritual guidance of one person, an unnamed anchoress, to whom Book I is addressed. Book II does not seem to address anyone in particular, and its more advanced teaching suggests that it may have been written several years after Book I. Hilton describes with authority and insight the spiritual development of the soul in very practical terms. Unusual for his time, the active and contemplative life are related so that the higher stages of prayer are not reserved for the enclosed, but are available to anyone willing to make the necessary effort. Thus the contemplative life is seen as a continuation and further development of the normal life of grace in the soul.

The foundation of the spiritual life is the re-establishment, or what Hilton calls the reforming, of the defaced image of God in the soul. This reform takes place in two stages. The first is a restoration "in faith," and the second is a reforming of "faith and feeling." These two stages are separated by the mystical "dark night" in which the soul becomes gradually detached from earthly things, and its eyes are opened and directed to things of the spirit:

The opening of the spiritual eyes is a glowing darkness and rich nothingness.... It may be called: Purity of soul and spiritual rest, inward stillness and peace of conscience, refinement of thought and integrity of soul, a lively consciousness of grace and solitude of heart, the wakeful sleep of the spouse and the tasting of heavenly joys, the ardor of love and brightness of light, the entry into contemplation and reformation of feeling...

Here the importance of affection is stressed, but feeling does not simply refer to an emotional state; it describes the awareness of the soul of the working of God's grace within it. Unlike Richard Rolle, Hilton warns against sensible, physical phenomena accompanying the spiritual life. The soul must recollect itself inwardly and remember its three original powers of memory, understanding and will—a created trinity which is made perfect in its mind, vision and love by the uncreated Trinity.

Hilton speaks of three degrees of contemplation. The first consists of the knowledge of God and such spiritual matters which can be attained by reason, reading and studying Christian teachings and scriptures. The second degree consists in affection and feeling, a love of God and great devotion. It is subdivided into two further stages where the lower may be reached by those leading an active life, whereas the higher stage is achieved only by those wholly devoted to the contemplative life who, after much physical and spiritual effort, can progress to the third and highest stage, characterized by "cognition and affection," the perfect knowledge and love of God linked to mystical union, as far as this is possible in the present life. The ultimate stage of perfection can be reached only in heaven.

Those who aim for a reform of both faith and feeling are like pilgrims on their way to the city of Jerusalem, the city of peace, which stands for

The Vision of the Lamb in Heaven, an illumination from the Lambeth Apocalypse (c.1260). The goal of the seeker is communion with the Godhead, attained by progress through degrees of contemplation. The mystery of the Incarnation, in which God became flesh in order to participate in the suffering of the world, was often represented by the sacrificial Lamb. (Lambeth Palace Library, London)

the ultimate stage of contemplation. Like all pilgrims, they must leave unnecessary things behind and overcome all kinds of obstacles:

> *A real pilgrim going to Jerusalem leaves his house and land, wife and children; he divests himself of all that he possesses in order to travel light and without encumbrances. Similarly, if you wish to be a spiritual pilgrim, you must divest yourself of all that you possess; that is, both of good deeds and bad, and leave them all behind you. Recognize your own poverty, so that you will not place any confidence in your own work; instead, always be desiring the grace of deeper love, and seeking the spiritual presence of Jesus. If you do this, you will be setting your heart wholly on reaching Jerusalem, and on nothing else.*

Jesus is seen as the guide on this pilgrimage. The desire for a reform of feeling comes from him. Loving Jesus and desiring oneness with him, the soul will enter the luminous darkness that forces out false love of the world. Knowledge of Jesus's humanity through the imagination can bring the soul to the light of Christ and create the deepest feeling, the most fervent love for God who is uncreated love. In a chapter entitled "How Jesus must be sought, desired, and found," Hilton writes:

> *...because the eyes of your spirit are not yet opened, I shall give you one word to express everything which you must seek and desire and find...and this word is "Jesus." I do not mean the letters "IHS" painted on a wall or written in a book, I do not mean the sounds of the word which you form with your tongue, I do not mean the name as it can be fixed in the heart.... through such exercises man in love may find Him, but here by "Jesus" I mean all goodness, everlasting wisdom, love and sweetness, your joy, your dignity and your eternal happiness, your God, your Lord and your salvation....*
>
> *....However much you know or feel of Him here in this life, He is still far above it; and therefore if you want to find the whole of Him as He is in the bliss of love, never cease whilst you live to long spiritually for Him.*

Through grace, the soul can rise in contemplation, withdraw into a secret chamber where it can see God, hear God's counsels and be wonderfully consoled. It is here that the soul, freed from worldly concerns, hears with spiritual joy the whisper of God. But once this grace is withdrawn, the soul sinks back into its state of natural weakness and ordinary dullness, only to wait for the grace of God's sweetness to return.

Christ as the Man of Sorrows on the Cross. Illumination from the
fifteenth-century English Lewkenor Book of Hours. For Hilton, emotion
and awareness combined in devotion to Jesus and contemplation of his
humanity. Through this, the soul was freed from worldly concerns and
able to rise to a higher spiritual plane. (Lambeth Palace Library, London)

Julian of Norwich (1342–c. 1423)

Until the mid-seventeenth century, Hilton, Rolle, and *The Cloud of Unknowing* were much better known than Julian of Norwich, whose work enjoyed none of their popularity. But today Julian is probably the best known of all the medieval English mystics. Her thought, though complex and profound, is expressed in a homely style, and her work is now one of the most accessible. Interest in Julian has experienced a great revival in recent years, not least through the contemporary "Julian meetings" dedicated to retreats and contemplation. But who was this famous medieval English woman mystic?

We know little about her personal life, except for what she tells us in her writing, supplemented by some information in wills found in the city archives of Norwich. She may first have joined a Benedictine community, but later lived alone as an anchoress in a cell or a little house-like structure attached to a church. Between the twelfth and thirteenth centuries, ninety-two anchoresses are known to have lived in England, compared to only twenty anchorites. The name "anchoress" does not mean that these women were "anchored" to a church, as the medievals supposed, but comes from the Greek word *anachorein,* meaning "to go apart." To live as an anchoress was the commitment to living a life of contemplation and prayer, to stay in one place until one's death, to follow certain rules and to live under the protection of the bishop. It was not meant to be a hard ascetic life, but one without luxury or disturbance, and dedicated to a deeply spiritual orientation. The anchoress was not without contact with the outside world, for visitors could come to seek counsel and a maid

would have brought food and water, cooked, and attended to the fire.

The anchoress of Norwich was probably given the name Julian because her cell was attached to the parish church of St. Julian at Conisford in Norwich. Before she became an anchoress, in May 1373, at the age of thirty and a half, Julian fell ill to the point of death and was given the last rites. But she then received a series of sixteen visions, and recovered from her illness. Shortly afterwards she wrote down her visions and the resulting work is entitled *Showings,* or *Revelations of Divine Love,* the first book known to be written by a woman in English. It exists in two versions, a short text of twenty-five chapters and a much longer text of eighty-six chapters. The first is thought to have been written immediately after the visions were received, whereas the second is the fruit of twenty years' meditation on the meaning of these visions and includes much editorial reworking.

Julian claims to write as a "simple unlettered creature," but this is merely a rhetorical device. Her work proves that, far from illiterate, she was a person of great literary skill and profound learning, with a good knowledge of the Latin Bible and the great mystical writers of the Western spiritual tradition. It is uncertain where she received her education, but as a young girl she may have been educated by the Benedictine nuns at the nearby priory at Carrow.

Julian's *Revelations* are a classic of mystical theology, containing one of the clearest yet most complex records of the life of a mystical soul. Julian had desired three graces from God: to have a recollection of Christ's Passion and see his sufferings on the cross, as had Mary his mother and "others who were Christ's lovers"; to have a bodily sickness when she was thirty; and to be given three wounds as God's gift–contrition, compassion and longing with all her will for God.

She vividly describes her illness, and how she was so sick that her mother stood by her bed and a priest placed a crucifix before her eyes. She felt that the lower half of her body was already dead and the upper part was beginning to die when suddenly all the pain left and her visions began. These visions were very physical, especially when she describes Christ's suffering; yet at the same time they were also very spiritual, and their powerful, inspiring theme is the greatness of God's love for us, enfolding us like "our clothing." God embraces, guides, and surrounds us with a love "so tender that he may never desert us."

Julian's visions are concerned with God, Christ, and the Trinity, but also with Mary, with Christ's death and ours, with prayer, and with the spiritual understanding of sin and Christ's victory over the devil. For her the soul is at home in God: "Greatly should we rejoice that God dwells in our soul—and rejoice yet more because our soul dwells in God. Our soul is created to be God's home, and the soul is at home in the uncreated God."

Julian also saw something small, "no bigger than a hazelnut," lying in her hand, and understood this to represent everything that is made by God. She marveled at it because it seemed so little that it could "suddenly fall into nothing." Yet she was assured that it lasts, and always will, because God loves it so much. Profoundly aware of God's love, Julian also knew of the existence of evil and sin, which she described as "the greatest pain that the soul can have." She tried to combine her deep experience of God's constant, steadfast love with the Church's teaching on sin, but said of God, "I saw him assign to us no kind of blame." God wishes to cure us of two kinds of sickness: impatience and despair. He is all wisdom and can do everything, he is all love and wishes to do everything. Julian's great experience of God who is all love finds expression in her profound trust that "All is well, and every kind of thing will be well."

Perhaps she had a deep love of her own mother, which influenced her teaching about the motherhood of God—a theme already found in St. Anselm, but much further developed by Julian, who speaks of God as our Mother as well as our Father: "God rejoices that he is our Father, and God rejoices that he is our Mother, and God rejoices that he is our true spouse, and that our soul is his beloved wife." It is particularly Christ who is "our Mother, brother and savior", "our kind Mother, our gracious Mother." Reflecting on this image, she writes:

> The Mother's service is nearest, readiest and surest…We wit that all our mother's bearing is the bearing of us to pain and dying: and what is this but that our Very Mother, Jesus, he—All-Love—beareth us to joy and endless living…. This fair lovely word Mother, it is so sweet and kind itself that it may verily be said of none but him; and to her that is very Mother of him and of all.

In about 1410, Julian received a visit from **Margery Kempe** (c. 1373-1440) in her cell at Norwich. Margery was another woman whose life was taken up by visions and revelations, with a deep devotion to the love of God, to Christ and

The Virgin as protectress, a woodcut from
The Mirour of Man's Salvacioun, a Middle English
translation of the *Speculum Humanae Salvationis*
(c. 1310-1324). Julian of Norwich taught the
"motherhood" of God, and her "showings"
included visions of the Virgin Mary. (London Library)

the Virgin. She came to seek Julian's counsel, for the reputation of the anchoress was such that her contemporaries sought her expert advice in spiritual matters. Margery's life and mystical experiences are in great contrast to Julian's. She traveled extensively and made pilgrimages to Jerusalem, Rome, Germany, and Spain. Her eventful life is reflected in a colorful account which she as an illiterate woman dictated to two clerks. Now known as *The Book of Margery Kempe,* this is the first spiritual autobiography in English, whose full text was only rediscovered in 1934. Opinions as to how far this relates genuinely mystical experiences greatly vary. David Knowles has described Margery as "filling every role from that of a saintly mystic to that of hysterical exhibitionist."

Margery's book is as emotional as it is vivid. Its stark descriptions give us an insight into the religious life of an ordinary fourteenth-century Christian, revealing a remarkable portrait of a strong-willed and forthright woman. While the book is not a treatise on contemplation, as are the works of Rolle, Hilton, or Julian, it makes its own contribution to the rich legacy of medieval mystics and includes as one of its major themes that God loves, is revealed to, and uses quite ordinary people in his many extraordinary ways of dealing with the world.

The great tradition of medieval mystics came to an end with the Reformation. After this long-drawn-out process of reform and renewal had created a new world and shaped new sensibilities, new mystical trends began to emerge again in different countries of Europe. Among Catholics, some of the old traditions prevailed but these were now adapted to the context of a different age making new demands on Christian life. Among Protestants the structures of medieval monasticism were rejected, and with them went much of the mystical heritage of the Middle Ages. But a new group of mystics soon emerged among Protestants—great, saintly figures, who combined a deeply mystical piety with life in the modern world. Thus the mystics of the early modern period in Europe present us with a different, but equally rich tradition of Christian spirituality focused on the search for perfection and loving union with God, expressed with great vigor and intensity, though embodied in very different forms from those found in the medieval Church.

CHAPTER FOUR

MYSTICS OF THE EARLY MODERN PERIOD

During the early modern period, just as in ages gone by, numerous Christians sought to follow the spirit of the Gospel, strive for the highest ideal of Christian perfection, and live a life of deep mystical spirituality. From the sixteenth century onward, however, much changed with the coming of the Protestant Reformation. Traditionally, during the Middle Ages and before, many mystics were either members of religious orders or priests in the Catholic Church. Scorning a world-denying asceticism, the Protestant reformers abandoned the monastic and sacerdotal traditions of the Church, so that much of the contemplative tradition also died out, only to be rediscovered in centuries to come. Because of these developments it is often thought that there are no more mystics among Protestants, but this is not so.

There were no institutional structures in Protestantism to hand down the contemplative mystical teachings and practices, as had been the case in the monasteries, although some of the reformers themselves appreciated the mystical tradition of the Catholic Church. Quite a few mystics continued to appear in different Protestant Churches, but they were now mainly lay people rather than monks or ministers of a particular Church. These new mystics were much more individualistic, stressing personal experience and enlightenment which sometimes brought them into conflict with the authorities of their own Church, as will be seen later.

The early modern period is also characterized by the sensibilities of a new age. The explorations of new continents and new scientific laws meant that Europe discovered new geographical and intellectual frontiers which greatly expanded the boundaries of both the outer world and the inner mind. The onset of the Enlightenment raised challenging questions for philosophy and theology which had a deep impact on the understanding and practice of

The Trinity, by El Greco (1541-1614). Early modern painters depicted traditional Christian themes such as the Trinity with a very different sensibility from that of medieval artists. The energy, elongation, and disturbing asymmetry of El Greco's style suggest the intensity of his mystical experience. (Prado, Madrid)

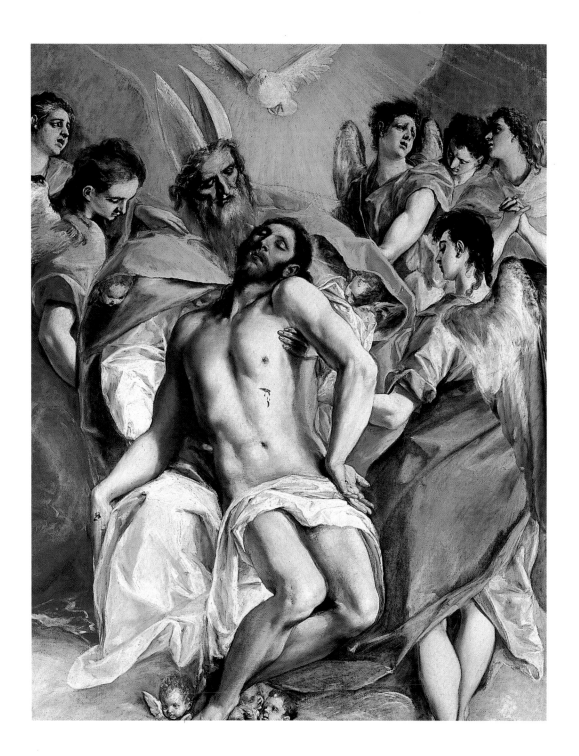

A woodcut showing the Creation of the World, from the Luther Bible,
c. 1530. Luther's German Bible was a landmark for the reformed
Christianity of the modern period, but its illustrations remained steeped
in the medieval world view. (Bible Society, London)

Christian spirituality and mysticism. New questions, opportunities and perspectives in all fields led to new emphases in combining contemplation and action as highest religious ideals.

We know of many modern mystics, both Catholic and Protestant, in France, Spain, Germany, and England, as well as in newly colonized territories overseas, but it is not possible to mention them all. Only the most important figures can be presented here, and these fall into three groups: Spanish, French, and Protestant.

In response to the Protestant Reformation there developed the Catholic Reform on the continent of Europe, sometimes called the "Counter-Reformation." With it arose the new Order of the Jesuits, founded by a Spaniard later known as St. Ignatius. Ignatian spirituality and practices deeply influenced the modern Catholic Church, as did the Carmelite mystics of Spain, among whom St. Teresa of Avila and St. John of the Cross are known as the mystics *par excellence*.

SPANISH MYSTICS

In post-Reformation Spain the religious temper was intense, but much of the newly emerging spirituality presented a dramatic break with the spiritual tradition of the early Church and the Middle Ages. Spanish mystical consciousness is marked by a mixture of activity, austerity, and ceaseless striving which developed during an age when the expansion of geographical frontiers brought with it an expansion of mission to take the Gospel to all corners of the globe.

Even before the Reformation, however, many important changes had occurred. The Black Death had led to much relaxed observance of monastic rules, and in the effort for a return to stricter observance more attention was paid to the inner life of prayer, which brought a new emphasis on the experience of the individual and a more subjective spirituality. Abundant literature on the interior life was made available. Instructions for methodical mental prayer were developed separately from the customary manuals on asceticism, and stressed that prayer, rightly pursued, led to pure love and union with God. The call to Christian perfection was addressed to all, not only to monastics, and the newly developed printing presses helped to disseminate the new teaching on prayer. In this way the search for union with God was brought out of the monasteries and extended to the laity. Such union was likened to two distinct fires becoming one fire, or to the way a drop of water falls into the sea and becomes one with it— comparisons which are not unlike those found in Hinduism.

A new emphasis was placed on following Christ externally and internally, and the call to follow his humanity produced a wealth of literature on his Passion and death. In fact, the Passion of Christ became the most frequent subject of meditation, and this has left a deep mark on Spanish religious art. The search for quiet contemplation produced the well-known formula *ne pensar nada,* "to think of nothing" and thereby to attend to the All.

This new spirituality began to emerge in Spain in the early sixteenth century, and suited a new age of travelers and explorers for whom the discipline of a monastery was unsuitable. It was given much impetus by the writings on prayer by such spiritual authors as Osuna, Laredo, and

St. Ignatius of Loyola, by Peter Paul Rubens (1577-1640). This splendid
painting shows Ignatius in full priestly robes with his well-known dedication
"to the greater glory of God. (Musée de Sibiu, Romania)

Palma, but it was also closely linked to the support given by the Catholic Church to work against the reformers of northern Europe. Specifically different Jesuit and Carmelite mystical spiritualities developed, each with its own characteristics. While the traditional monastic orders carried on their spiritual teachings and practices as before, the Jesuit Order produced an altogether new kind of spirituality and mystical orientation. The example of its founder, Ignatius, also created a new kind of asceticism linked to activity, travel, and a new engagement with human reality, rather than self-imposed mortification and withdrawal from the world.

Ignatian spirituality, so influential in the modern development of the Catholic Church, has been described as "contemplation in action." It centers upon the exhortation to find God in all things, not just in prayer or the solitude of the cloister. This world-affirming quality is the hallmark of modernity, and represents a break with medieval piety. The inner call for loving intimacy with the Divine is now primarily expressed through ministry in the world and service to others and the Church. This decidedly active character of Jesuit spirituality and mysticism is clearly visible in the life of St. Ignatius of Loyola himself.

St. Ignatius Loyola (1491-1556)

Born into a noble family living at the castle of Loyola in northern Spain, Ignatius first embarked on a military career, but was wounded during the siege of Pamplona in 1521. During his long convalescence he underwent a profound religious conversion. He then spent much time in prayer and was deeply influenced by two medieval works, *The Life of Christ* and *The Golden Legend,* dealing with the lives of saints. Following this he devoted a year to prayer and mortification at Manresa, experiencing both temptations and numerous mystical insights. He became convinced that he had been called by God to be a soldier for Christ, instead of working as a soldier for the king. During this time he composed the substance of his *Spiritual Exercises,* which record his spiritual experiences for the help of others.

These *Exercises*, which use knightly and military imagery, express essentially a spirituality of service. One of the most important documents in the history of Christian spirituality, this book is a manual of discipline which teaches the life of the Spirit to others and asks the Christian disciple to reflect continuously on the life, death, and resurrection of Christ.

Ignatius soon realized that he needed a formal education in theology, and after studying in several cities in Spain, he arrived at the University of Paris, where he studied from 1528 to 1535. Here he gathered a group of companions around him with whom he eventually founded the Society of Jesus, one of the most significant religious orders in the history of the Catholic Church. They took their religious vows in 1534 and were ordained priests in 1537. By 1540 Pope Paul III approved the Jesuits as an official Order of the Church, with Ignatius of Loyola as its first "general," or leader. From then on Ignatius spent most of his remaining life in or near Rome. He died there in 1556 and was canonized in 1622.

Ignatius wrote the *Spiritual Exercises* over several years and revised them throughout his life. They not only became the guide for the

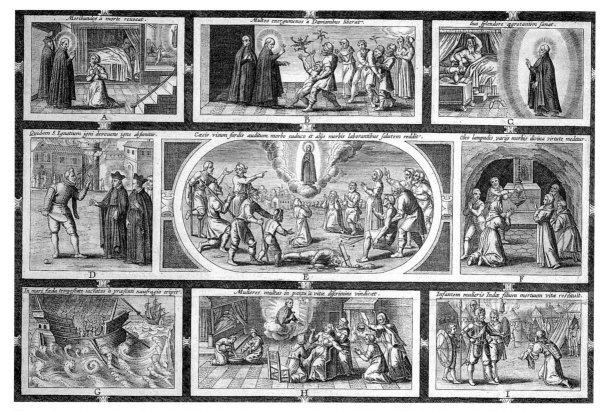

The wonders and miracles performed by St. Ignatius of Loyola, engraved by Jean Galle, c. 1600. Loyola's mystical insight found expression in active engagement with the world. (Private Collection)

spiritual life of the Jesuits, but are used by many people as a handbook for spiritual renewal. They outline a program of progressive spiritual exercises to be followed during four weeks, and appear rather rationalistic in their language and arguments. These carefully organized instructions seem at first to have little to do with mystical experience, yet the ultimate goal of the *Exercises* is the first-hand experience of God, "to allow the creator to work directly on the creature."

Whereas earlier mystics saw the goal of Christian perfection as contemplation and divinization, Ignatius of Loyola was the first of the moderns to stress that the primary aim of the spiritual life is the identification of the human will with the divine will, regardless of experiential effects. Thus the overall result is a much more practical orientation, a spirituality geared to Christian ministry and the tasks of daily life, although the *Exercises* are also concerned with such themes as the "election" of God and the discernment of spirits.

Ignatius points to an "election," an ordering of life "for the greater service and praise" of God. To make spiritual growth happen, continued self-examination is necessary and the imitation of Christ is the essence of Christian discipleship. One can no doubt detect here the influence of the late medieval tradition of the *devotio moderna* and its principal document, *The Imitation of Christ* of St. Thomas à Kempis. Ignatius had a special fondness for this work and shared its view that all devotion is a means to conform to the image of Christ. The *devotio moderna* created an influential literature, concerned with different methods of prayer which were organized into regular exercizes. Prayer was said to lead to greater intimacy with God, and meditation on the incarnation of God in Christ prepares the soul for spiritual experience culminating in the experience of divine love.

One group went to extremes in practicing this love as a complete abandonment to God, declaring all prayers, rites, and ceremonies as useless whilst seeking ecstasy and other extraordinary phenomena. This Spanish group, called the *Alumbrados*, or Illuminists, was condemned by the Inquisition; even Ignatius was suspected of following their forbidden practices and was interrogated about them.

It is especially at the end of Loyola's *Exercises*, in the section entitled "Contemplation for Obtaining Love," that we find the essence of Christian mystical life expressed. The union between the human being and God is one of love, where each gives and each receives in the mutual interchange between lover and beloved. An offering of great love and affection is expressed in Ignatius' prayer:

Take, O Lord, and receive all my liberty, my memory, my understanding, and my entire will, all that I have and possess. Thou hast given all these things to me; to Thee, O Lord, I restore them: all are Thine, dispose of them all according to Thy will. Give me Thy love and Thy grace, for this is enough for me.

Ignatius achieved this surrender to God in an eminent degree during his life and experienced a deep sense of the divine presence within him. There was a strongly Trinitarian aspect to his personal mysticism. He emphasized the individuality of the three persons of the Trinity, Father, Son, and Holy Spirit, and the dynamism of his spirituality was particularly due to the sense of divine action within his own being. Even during his lifetime he was revered for his union with God, which seemed to manifest itself to all who met him.

Ignatius' newly founded Order was particularly active in education and mission, carried out with the intention that everything was undertaken for the greater glory of God. Travel and displacement were part of the ministry of service to others. Such service took precedence over the chanting of the Divine Office and the vow of stability which had characterized the traditional monastic communities. Thus the Jesuits represented a complete contrast to the way of life pursued by the monks in older orders.

Building on the foundations laid by Ignatius and his *Exercises*, several other Jesuits from Spain, France, and Italy developed detailed instructions on how to attain the different stages of Christian life and how to relate the methods of the *Exercises* to the three traditional ways of mysticism—the purgative, illuminative, and unitive. The Jesuit Order introduced new spiritual practices such as retreats, spiritual direction, and confraternities of various kinds, all of which helped to spread new forms of spirituality and popular piety in early modern Europe.

Another towering mystical figure of the sixteenth century, the golden age of Spanish spirituality, was Teresa of Avila, one of the greatest women mystics of the Roman Catholic Church and celebrated author of highly influential spiritual classics on the mystical life.

St. Teresa of Avila (1515-82)

Teresa de Cepeda y Ahumada was of mixed Jewish and Christian background. She had two sisters and nine brothers, but at the age of fourteen lost her mother. Despite her father's opposition, she decided to become a Carmelite nun when she was barely twenty-one. She entered the Carmelite Convent of the Incarnation at Avila, and took the name Teresa of Jesus. The change in diet and way of life so much affected her health that she soon fell seriously ill and remained an invalid for several years. It was during this time that she developed a great love of mental prayer, especially after reading Francisco de Osuna's *Third Spiritual Alphabet*. She followed this book's instructions about the prayer of quiet or recollection, and after a short time she received the gift of passive prayer of quiet and union. Yet, after her recovery from illness, she stopped praying and vacillated for almost twenty years between worldly and spiritual aspirations, trying to find a balance between her relationship to the world and that to God. This deep division within her was eventually overcome when she experienced a stunning conversion, resulting in an intense journey of prayer and active religious reform

over the remaining years of her life.

Her mysticism was influenced by the spirituality and methods of the Jesuits and Franciscans, but given her partly Jewish background, her thinking was also affected by Jewish Kabbalistic mysticism, elements of which can be detected in her writings. Teresa possessed extraordinary administrative and literary talents, but no theological training, and her ardent love of God influenced all her activities. Her ascetical doctrine is accepted as the classical exposition of the contemplative life, and her spiritual writings are among the most widely read. They are notable for their simplicity and passionate interest in the detailed description of the human experience of prayer, while her life was full of activity, reforming and founding convents and traveling to many parts of Spain. Her life represents an almost ideal balance between contemplation and action, so that it has been said that seldom have the activities of Martha and Mary been so well combined as in the personality of St. Teresa.

The Carmelite Order had originated in Palestine, with hermits living at the foot of Mount Carmel. By the thirteenth century members of the Order had migrated and established houses all over Europe, so that gradually their original, strict rule became rather lax and was in need of reform. Like many other Carmelite houses, the Convent of the Incarnation at Avila was lax in its observance. Teresa considered it spiritually harmful that the convent was not fully enclosed, but was so open to the world. After her conversion she developed the idea to set up a convent of Discalced, or Barefoot, nuns who would observe the strict original Carmelite rule. She encountered

St. Teresa of Avila, by Juan de la Miseria (c. 1526-1616). Teresa was one of the most fervent Christian mystics, who combined to an unusual degree the depths of mystical experience with a life of great creative activity. (Convent of St. Teresa, Avila, Spain)

The Convent of St. Joseph in Avila, Spain, was the first of the many reformed Carmelite convents founded by St. Teresa.

considerable difficulties, but eventually founded the Convent of St. Joseph in Avila, followed by the foundation of many other reformed houses, including some for men. It was during this work of reform that she first met the younger Juan de Yepes, later known as St. John of the Cross, who became a close collaborator, adviser, and friend.

Teresa undertook many exhausting journeys, described in her *Life*, and died in 1582 while traveling between Burgos and Avila. She was canonized in 1622, in the same year as Ignatius of Loyola, Frances Xavier, and others. In 1814 she was made the national saint of Spain. Only in the twentieth century was she declared a woman Doctor of the Church, together with Catherine of Siena.

Teresa's works include her *Life, The Way of Perfection,* the *Foundations, The Interior Castle,* and a number of poems and letters. She has described in detail how her mystical experiences developed as a result of her prayer practices. She often contemplated the picture of Christ within her and sometimes, when reading, there would come to her "such a feeling of the presence of God as made it impossible for me to doubt that He was within me, or that I was totally engulfed in Him."

In her *Life,* Teresa has described the four stages of mental prayer through which she passed, culminating in ecstatic union with God. But she also speaks of a state beyond union, a "rapture, or elevation, or flight of the spirit," a sudden, passive experience which she compares to being borne on the wings of an eagle. Such rapture is irresistible, but it is a transitory experience from which the soul returns to the ordinary world. The highest experience of mystical union, the "spiritual marriage" of the soul and God, of which she speaks at length in *The Interior Castle,* always leads her back to active service of God among her fellow human beings.

Teresa's trances, visions, locutions, and ecstasies counted for little to her by comparison with this active realization of Christian spirituality. Her advice to beginners is very practical and homely. She compares the life of prayer to the making of a garden in which the Lord may take delight. For the plants to grow to their full beauty, the garden has to be watered:

The magnificent sculpture of the ecstasy of St. Teresa by Gianlorenzo Bernini (1598-1680) is probably one of the best-known representations of any Christian mystic. Teresa described her ecstatic inner experience as being engulfed by God. (Santa Maria della Vittoria, Rome)

It seems to me that the garden can be watered in four ways: by taking the water from a well, which costs us great labor; or by a water-wheel and buckets, when the water is drawn by a windlass...it is less laborious than the other and gives more water; or by a stream or a brook, which waters the ground much better...or by heavy rain, when the Lord waters it with no labor of ours, a way incomparably better than any of those which have been described." Similarly, the beginner in prayer has to make great efforts and endure many trials, but these diminish until the Lord freely bestows the greatest gifts on the soul.

The fullest account of Teresa's spiritual journey is found in *The Interior Castle*. The castle is an image of the soul where God takes his delight, an image which came to Teresa during prayer when she tried to explain what happens on the soul's journey to God. The castle contains seven mansions with many different rooms, and the beginner enters by means of mental prayer and then travels through the different mansions, each of which represents a different stage of prayer life. The sixth mansion represents the stage of spiritual betrothal, a transition to the fullness of union with God experienced in the spiritual marriage of the seventh mansion.

It was bold of Teresa to affirm the necessity of mental prayer, for this kind of prayer was associated with the heretical *Alumbrados,* or Illuminists, persecuted by the Inquisition, and many of them were women. For Teresa, mental prayer was the beginning of the path to new ways of understanding, to the tasting of the deep mysteries of faith, which included the indwelling presence of the Trinity and of Jesus Christ in his humanity and divinity, as well as insights into sin

and grace, the Church and the sacraments. Her visions were both spiritual and physical, and she eventually experienced the grace of perfect union with Christ so that she became inseparable from him "as when a little stream enters the sea." Although Teresa was given extraordinary mystical favors, she did not consider these as essential for spiritual growth:

The highest perfection obviously does not consist in interior delights or in great raptures or in visions or in the spirit of prophecy but in having our will so much in conformity with God's will that there is nothing we know he wills that we do not want with all our desire, and in accepting the bitter as happily as we do the delightful when we know that His Majesty desires it.

Teresa's fervent mysticism has inspired countless men and women, from her own day to the present. Among the first who felt her powerful influence and attraction was her younger contemporary, St. John of the Cross, who is perhaps even more celebrated than Teresa herself. His work achieved such perfect fusion of intellectual, poetic, and mystical insights and soared to such mystical heights that he has been called "the mystic's mystic."

St. John of the Cross (1542-91)

Born as Juan de Yepes into a poor family living not far from Avila, his exceptional intellectual and spiritual gifts were recognized by a devout patron who provided for his education. Juan studied at a Jesuit school, but entered the Carmelite Order. He was sent to study at the famous University of Salamanca, and became

The collection of the most precious manuscripts in the Great Library at the Pontifical University of Salamanca, Spain, where Juan de Yepes studied theology before his ordination.

known as John of the Cross. Soon after his ordination in 1567 he met Teresa of Avila, then fifty-two years old, and this encounter determined the rest of his life.

Teresa urged him to join the Carmelite Reform, which he did. But through this he became much involved in the conflicts between the unreformed and the reformed parts of his Order. Those who were opposed to stricter and more ascetic observances resorted to force, taking John prisoner, interrogating, flogging, and incarcerating him for more than eight months in prison in Toledo, where he was subjected to great hard-

Engraving by Lucas Vorsterman (1595-1675) showing St. John of the Cross kneeling in prayer before a painting of Christ bearing the cross. (Bibliothèque National, Paris)

ships and deprivations. Yet this imprisonment was decisive in his development as a mystic, because, stripped of everything, he was entirely thrown back upon God. He began to write poems on small scraps of paper which are now considered some of the greatest lyrical poetry in the Spanish language.

He eventually escaped from prison, probably with the help of one of the jailers, and spent most of the rest of his life as a superior and spiritual director in Andalusia. The greater

part of his writing, undertaken in Granada, consists of extensive commentaries on his mystical poems explaining the way to union with God.

His three most famous poems are "The Spiritual Canticle," "*En una noche obscura*" (the "Dark Night" poem), and "The Living Flame of Love." His books *The Ascent of Mount Carmel* and *The Dark Night of the Soul* are commentaries on the "Dark Night" poem; the other commentaries have the same titles as the poems.

The mystical works of St. John of the Cross are more appreciated, possibly, in the twentieth century than ever before. For a long time his mixing of the lyrical language of poetry with the conceptual language of theology was found difficult, and gave rise to a lack of trust in his writings. John celebrates the mystery of God's transcendence and immanence by describing it as a pattern of darkness and light. The union with God, the goal of all spiritual life, is a union of the deepest love. But God is hidden and must be sought. This search for the Beloved is like the ascent of a mountain or an escape at night, a gradual journey with stages of progression and regression until the soul is completely transformed into God just as a log of wood is transformed when placed into fire.

John distinguishes two "nights of the soul," the night of the senses when the sensual part of the soul is purified, and the night of the spirit, given to only a few, when the soul undergoes the deepest purgation through God's inflowing into the soul, removing all ignorance and imperfection, leading to illumination and union. God is in fact the divine lover who searches the soul more than the soul seeks God, a lover "who, in the omnipotence of His fathomless love, absorbs the soul in Himself more efficaciously and forcibly than a torrent of fire would devour the drop of morning dew."

St. John's mysticism is in the great apophatic tradition, following the *via negativa*, whereby the soul detaches herself increasingly from the specific and knowable until, in utter detachment, she knows only that which is dark, which is God. The "dark night" is the image for this journey of detachment and purgation consisting of the active and passive purgation of the senses and the spirit until the soul is transformed into God and conforms completely to

God's will. John was probably familiar with the writings of Denys the Areopagite, Eckhart and Ruusbroec, but his own works provide a more precise and comprehensive description of the way of unknowing than earlier texts.

His mystical map assumes that God is totally other than the soul, yet can be known by the soul and loved in a most intimate union. It is in fact the purpose of Christian life to seek such mystical union so that all Christians are called to ascend the mount where God lives. Here are some stanzas from "The Spiritual Canticle," praising the beauty of the Beloved:

The ornate buildings of the ancient University of Salamanca, overlooked by the city's great cathedral. In the courtyard stands a statue of the scholar Luis de León (1528-91), who taught at the University and first translated the Song of Songs into Spanish.

My Beloved is the mountains,
And lonely wooded valleys,
Strange islands,
And resounding rivers,
The whistling of love-stirring breezes,
The tranquil night

At the time of the rising dawn
Silent music,
Sounding solitude
The supper that refreshes, and deepens love.

The examples of John of the Cross and Teresa were followed by the Carmelites who succeeded them. Inspired by the writings of these two great mystics, their followers systematized their teachings on mental prayer and the mystical life. By the second half of the seventeenth century a considerable number of scholastic treatises on what was now called "mystical theology" appeared in Spain, Portugal, and France. The thought of the Spanish mystics acted like a living stream, feeding the spiritual life of Western Christianity. It deeply influenced and shaped the spirituality of the Roman Catholic Church in the modern period, not least in France, where a "French School" of mystics developed soon afterwards.

FRENCH MYSTICS

The Spanish mystics are generally better known than the French mystics, yet during the sixteenth and seventeenth centuries the Catholic Church in France produced several outstanding figures who bear strong witness to the continuing attraction of the mystical life. Something like a mystical renaissance took place in France after the works of Teresa of Avila and Catherine of Genoa, followed by those of John of the Cross, were translated into French. These mystical writers inspired a group of French Catholics to formulate an approach to the spiritual life which, together with the teaching of the Jesuits, became normative in the centuries that followed and still represents what most modern Catholics think of as traditional spirituality.

The great age of French spirituality opens with an Englishman, Benedict of Canfield, a man from Essex who had converted to Catholicism, studied at the English College at Douai, and become a Franciscan in 1587. He showed unusual spiritual gifts, but published his *Rule of Perfection* only towards the end of his life, in 1609. His example exercized such a formative influence on the rise of French mysticism that Benedict has been called "the master of the masters" of the seventeenth-century French mystics and spiritual writers.

Particularly marked was his influence on Madame Acarie (1566-1618), a devoted wife and mother of six children, who had originally wished to be a nun. She possessed a naturally religious temperament and experienced raptures and ecstasies. Her life was deeply affected by Augustine's saying, "He is indeed a miser to whom God is not enough." She became detached from earthly affections and under the influence of Benedict of Canfield, who had assured her that her raptures came from God, she gathered an extraordinary group of people around her, a kind of spiritual salon in the Rue des Juifs in Paris.

A portrait of Cardinal Pierre de Bérulle, by Frère François, 1859. The seventeenth-century spiritual writer, reformer and diplomat exercized much influence in France, both during his lifetime and afterwards. (Maison de Lazaristes, Paris)

These regular gatherings became the focus of spiritual life in the French capital at that time.

Madame Acarie's advice as spiritual counselor was much sought after. Her influence extended even to the reformation of religious houses. Reading the works of St. Teresa led her to establish the Order of the Discalced Carmelites in France, with a core group of nuns brought over from Spain. She is said to have received the stigmata, and contemporaries praised "her great inwardness and familiarity with God," mentioning that "her countenance, like that of Moses, was wont to become wholly luminous."

It has been said that there is something peculiarly French in having a mystical movement launched in a salon with the hostess attending to both the business affairs of her husband and the conversations of the spiritual masters of her time. Prominent among her guests and one of the chief founders of the "French School" of spirituality was Pierre de Bérulle (1575-1629), who had been educated by the Jesuits and was deeply attracted to Madame Acarie, whose raptures he had witnessed at first hand. Reformer of the clergy and founder of the French Oratory, he became Madame Acarie's spiritual director and closely collaborated with her in bringing the Carmelite Order to France. Bérulle combined his interest in the spiritual and mystical with a close involvement in ecclesiastical and secular politics. His spiritual writings contain detailed descriptions of the cultivation of the interior life.

Important debates took place among the French mystics regarding the nature of the spiritual life, of prayer and contemplation, the role of grace in the life of the mystic, and the relationship between mysticism and social action. Some advocated a very pessimistic outlook on life; others stressed its goodness and attraction. For a time quietism became fashionable; this was an extreme form of contemplative devotion in which spiritual indifference, passivity, and extinction of the will were cultivated. Others, by contrast, advocated an active spirituality which found the presence of God in all things. Such an active orientation is found in the works of Francis de Sales, whose life blended pastoral and mystical concerns. Francis showed great respect for Madame Acarie without being directly involved with her circle in Paris, far away from his own field of activity.

St. Francis de Sales (1567-1622)

Francis was born into a noble family from Savoy, and was educated at a Jesuit college in Paris. This was followed by higher studies, first in Paris and then at the University of Padua, where he read law. After briefly practicing as a lawyer he turned to religion and, in 1593, was ordained as priest in Annecy, the chief town of his native Savoy. Annecy was also the place to which the bishop's See of Geneva had been moved in 1535, along with the monasteries that had been expelled from Geneva during the Reformation.

Francis soon became the provost of the cathedral chapter. As a staunch defender of the Catholic faith he was active in the struggle against Calvinism and helped to reconvert a whole region of France back to Catholicism. By 1602 he was Bishop of Geneva, enjoying a great reputation as preacher, spiritual writer, and director. It was through listening to his Lenten sermons in Dijon that Jeanne de Chantal first met him in 1604. She placed herself under his

A seventeenth-century engraving of the greatly influential French devotional writer, Francis de Sales, who spoke of the spiritual fire and flame of Christian love dedicated to the service of others.

spiritual direction and eventually they together founded the Visitation Order, an enclosed order for nuns which grew rapidly in their lifetime.

Francis de Sales left a considerable body of writings, consisting of texts explaining Catholic doctrine and arguing against Calvinists, personal letters, sermons, and diocesan administrative documents. But his great reputation as a spiritual writer and mystic rests primarily on two deeply personal works which celebrate a fervent devotion and love of God. When he published his *Introduction to the Devout Life* in 1609 as a spiritual guide for those who live in the world rather than in the cloister, this book caught the religious sensibilities of his age. It became immediately so famous that edition after edition was printed. The dowager queen of France even gave it as a gift in jeweled binding to James I of England.

It was his intention, Francis said in the preface, "to instruct those who live in towns, in families, or at court." He wanted to prove that "a vigorous and resolute soul may live in the world without being infected by any of its moods, may discover sweet springs of piety amidst its salt waters, and may fly through the flames of earthly lusts without burning the wings of the holy desires of a devout life." For him devotion is an intense form of love: "Charity and devotion differ no more from one another than does flame from the fire. Charity is spiritual fire and when it bursts into flame, it is called devotion."

The ardor of love is also the central theme of his magisterial *Treatise on the Love of God.* Completed in 1616 this book, like its more modest predecessor, met again with instant celebrity. It was repeatedly reprinted; when the first English translation of 1630 was made, it was based on the eighteenth French printing. Francis wrote so much out of personal experience that it could be said his works are nothing but his spiritual correspondence writ large. His *Introduction* is mainly based on spiritual advice given to several women, especially to Marie de Charmoisy. The tenderness of friendship and the deeply personal engagement of his spiritual counsel mark his writing with a warmth and directness which touch the heart as few other spiritual writers do. It is this experiential and profoundly personal tone which resonated with his readers and still appeals today.

The *Introduction* argued that the heights of spiritual life could be pursued without withdrawing from the world. In the treatise *On the Love of God,* Francis speaks of the progress and perfection of love and the soul's union with God. This work shows how much he wrote from his own experience of mystical union.

Madonna and Child, by Jacques Blanchard (1600-38). It was through prayer to Our Lady that Francis de Sales experienced the love of God and his fellow human beings. His mystical sensibility was shaped by several feminine influences, not least that of Jeanne de Chantal, whose friendship and spiritual support were a great inspiration to him. (Private Collection)

At the basis of Francis' life lies a single experience which shaped his life and spirituality. As a young man at college with the Jesuits he experienced six weeks of mental torment when, unsure of himself, he was haunted by the fear that God had predestined him to go to hell, without any hope of salvation. Eventually, when praying in a church to Our Lady, the troubles left him and he felt entirely healed from his terror. He now became deeply assured that God has friendship, love, and salvation for all, and extends his abundance of grace to every single person. Throughout these dark weeks he learned a principle he never forgot: "to have compassion on the infirmities of others," and that "to live a Christian life, one must possess charity."

His spirituality from then on was an ongoing quest, so that his *Introduction* is presented as a pilgrim's progress toward a life of devotion. The interior life is one of journey and development toward the incomprehensible mystery that is God, a God we speak of in many names and images. Francis refers to God above all in terms of divine majesty, but this majesty gives way to a God who is also profoundly maternal. He likens God to a mother nursing her child, embodying the deepest form of unconditioned, active, and most ardent love.

For Francis, prayer is loving conversation with God, moving from discursive meditation to the simple gaze of contemplation. The special grace of God draws the soul into the deepest quiet which is a repose "so deep in its tranquillity that the whole soul and all its powers remain as if sunk in sleep." Such union can go so deep that the experience of love rises into ecstasy. Here the influence of St. Teresa is evident when Francis writes:

The Blessed Mother Teresa effectively says that when union attains this perfection of keeping us held and fastened to our Lord, it is the same as spiritual rapture, transport, or suspension, of spirit; it is called union, suspension or transport only when it is brief, whereas when prolonged, it is called ecstasy or rapture.

Whereas many other spiritual writers in seventeenth-century France held a pessimistic view of the human being, stressing sin and abnegation, Francis de Sales believed in the inherent goodness of human nature. Human beings have a natural inclination to love God, due to the correspondence between divine goodness and human souls which bear some kind of divine imprint or spark. God holds us by this goodness as in some way linked to Himself "as little birds by a string, by which he can draw us when it pleases His Compassion". Francis does not speak about the "ground" of the soul, like the Rhenish mystics, but refers to the "mountain top" of the soul, the utmost summit where self ends and God begins, a no-place which is yet a place, a dwelling-place that can be reached only by an all-transforming movement of love.

Pastoral and mystical elements are sensitively blended in Francis de Sales' spirituality, which had an enormous influence on the French elite of his time and continued to spread further after his death in 1622 as specifically "Salesian" spirituality. By 1665 Francis was already declared a saint, and over two centuries later, in 1877, he was the first writer in French to be named a Doctor of the Church, a title bestowed on saints whose writings enjoy special authority. Later still, in 1923, he was made patron saint of writers.

Many commentators on St. Francis de Sales have noticed the emphasis given to interior growth and spiritual development in his work. It is thought that the depth of this trend is directly due to his direction of Jeanne de Chantal, and his own inner growth resulting from their deep, abiding friendship

St. Jeanne de Chantal (1572-1641)

Jeanne Françoise Frémyot was born into an aristocratic family in Dijon. She showed strong religious inclinations, but was given in an arranged marriage to Baron de Rabutin-Chantal. Thus she lived a full and active married life for many years, bringing up four children. In 1601 her husband was killed in a hunting accident and she was left a widow. Her father-in-law threatened to disinherit her children if she did not reside with him, his mistress and his illegitimate children, a situation which caused great anxieties in Jeanne, but she tried to overcome these by drawing on the strength of her faith.

Three years after her husband's death she met Francis de Sales, who became her spiritual director and guide. They began a long correspondence which reflects much candor and warmth, and is permeated by gentleness and a genuine desire for spiritual freedom. A beautiful friendship developed between the two, mutually nourishing their inner development and spiritual growth towards God, but also their ability to perceive the needs of others and achieve common ideals.

In 1610, when Jeanne's eldest daughter was married and her fourteen-year-old son provided for, she took her two other daughters to Annecy where, together with Francis de Sales, she founded the Order of the Visitation, or Visitandines. This new women's order was based on the spirit of Francis' *Introduction to the Devout Life* and was begun with the intent "that no great severity shall prevent the feeble and the weak from joining it, there to devote themselves to the perfection of the divine love." Members of the order pledged to devote themselves to cultivating this divine love and to seeking hiddenness in God. In indifference to self, they sought a simple practice of the Presence of God by complete abandonment to his Providence.

Jeanne de Chantal became the head of the new order, and Francis its spiritual director. Out of his work with the women religious of the Visitation monastery of Mary in Annecy grew Francis's great guide to the mystical life, the *Treatise on the Love of God*. As he tells his readers:

> I must explain to you that we have in this city a community of young women and widows who have retired from the world so as to live together with one mind in God's service under the protection of his most holy Mother... Frequently I have tried to repay them by dispensing the holy word and I have delivered it to them both in public sermons and in spiritual conferences... A large part of what I now share with you, I owe to this blessed community.

The order had been in existence for six years when Francis wrote this. By the time he died in 1622, thirteen different houses of the Visitation Order existed in France. His death left Jeanne de Chantal deeply bereaved, and her sense of loss was further intensified when her son died in battle in 1627. But her activity did not diminish.

Engraving by Darodes of Jeanne de Chantal in *Les Saintes Femmes*, after a painting by Duval le Camus, nineteenth century. Under the direction of Francis de Sales, Jeanne founded a new women's order, the Visitandines, dedicated to the intense love of God and the care of the poor and sick.

She founded many further religious houses, and by the time she died in 1641 their number had increased to eighty-six.

The Visitation Order had been founded for charitable work, for visiting and caring for the sick and poor in their homes, as well as for prayer. But after the first five years of such work, the founders were obliged to accept the tradition of a cloistered life, a rule of strict enclosure, because this was considered indispensable for the life of religious women at that time. This basic change of orientation meant that Francis's original ideal of practicing spirituality in the world was once again constrained by the cloister.

Jeanne de Chantal's love of God was inseparable from service to the sick and poor. During the plague of 1628 she was even able to transform her monastery in Annecy into a hospital. Her devotion to God focused on "a simple beholding and realizing His divine presence, in which I felt utterly lost, absorbed, and at rest in Him." But in the later years of her life she experienced much spiritual dryness, her own dark night of the soul, when she could only remember the consciousness of the presence of God, rather than experience it directly.

The struggles of Jeanne's life, her married love and long-term friendship with men, her sense of the loss of loved ones, her capable administration and teaching, and her deep spiritual wisdom left a spiritual legacy which has appealed to many and is of great interest to women today. Her themes of "spiritual nudity" before God or the "death of ourselves for the sake of love" and the complete abandonment to God's will can be a source of strength at a time when so many traditional religious securities have been lost. Yet certain elements of her stark asceticism of self-renunciation can also be disturbing. But there can be no doubt that in spite of being severely constrained by her own gender role expectations and those of her contemporaries, Jeanne affirmed a full life for herself and reached great spiritual maturity in her deep and utter love for God. Unfortunately we have to learn about her development mostly from the writings of others, especially from the correspondence of St. Francis de Sales, because Jeanne destroyed almost all her letters to him. But by 1767 she was declared a saint in her own right.

Sketch of the young Blaise Pascal by a family friend, Jean Domat. A brilliant scientist and mathematician, Pascal was an intensely mystical person who exercised a lasting spiritual influence through his book *Pensées*. (Collection Philippe Barrès, Paris)

There are several other mystical figures of seventeenth-century France who might be considered here, for example the brilliant scientist and fervent believer **Blaise Pascal** (1623-62), who left us a moving text about his profoundly mystical experience of encountering the living "God of Abraham, God of Isaac, God of Jacob," not the God "of the philosophers and scholars." His reputation as a mystic rests almost entirely on his *Pensées,* published posthumously as an apology of the Christian faith addressed to the sceptics of his age.

In contrast to Pascal's brilliant genius with his ecstatic experience is the simple testimony of **Brother Lawrence** (1611-91), who perceived

God in a moment of abrupt intuition in an unecstatic manner as an abiding presence in his life. His simple way to holiness, rooted in his deep love for God, is expressed in *The Practice of the Presence of God,* the spiritual heritage of an unlearned Carmelite lay brother loved and cherished by many people.

Much the same teaching as Brother Lawrence's practice of the presence of God, adapted to a later, more complex age, was given by the French Jesuit **Jean Pierre de Caussade** (1675-1751) in his book *Abandonment to Divine Providence.* This consists of spiritual advice written for the nuns of the Visitation convent in Nancy, and is dependent in its teaching on John of the Cross and Francis de Sales. This work, well known only since the late nineteenth century, sums up the theme of self-abandonment so prominent among French Catholic mystics of the seventeenth and eighteenth centuries.

PROTESTANT MYSTICS

Protestantism is often better known for its suspicion of mysticism, rather than its support of it. Yet Protestant reformers were not indifferent to the mystical element in Christianity. Several of the founders of Protestantism and later Protestant divines were familiar with the mystical works of their Catholic predecessors. Much of the genius of Protestantism is expressed in hymns, creatively combining the art of music with religion in a way which powerfully underscores a deeply mystical Protestant piety and a great yearning for God's love and intimate presence. This is especially true of the two Wesleys, John and Charles, the founders of Methodism.

Triptych by Lucas Cranach (1472-1553). The central panel is a painting of the Last Supper, with Luther among the Apostles. On the left panel Philip Melanchthon performs a baptism assisted by Luther; on the right panel Luther makes his confession; below, Luther delivers a sermon. Reformers such as Melanchthon and Luther set a different tone for Christian spirituality, but the fervor of their faith still left room for the development of a deeply felt mystical piety among Protestant Christians. (Altarpiece in the Church of St. Marien, Wittenberg, Germany)

The Protestant Reformation created many different Protestant Churches in Europe, but these did not possess the necessary institutional and doctrinal structures to support the growth of mysticism in the way that medieval Catholicism had done through its monasteries and convents. It is true that many Protestants, especially Calvinists, have been strongly anti-mystical. But for all the Protestant hostility to traditional Catholic doctrine and practice, there remained a need to develop a personal spiritual relationship with God. Many different groups of spiritual seekers developed who eschewed the externals of religion and focused their search on God as the Beloved.

Much of this search continued to have links with earlier Catholic teachings on spirituality, and especially with the mystical tradition of the Middle Ages. Some think that only the Society of Friends or Quakers, described by Evelyn Underhill as "that great experiment in corporate mysticism," can claim genuine mystics, such as George Fox and John Woolman.

But even the Calvinist Jonathan Edwards can be counted among Protestant mystics, as can the Anglican poets George Herbert, Henry Vaughan and Thomas Traherne. Protestant mysticism is typically individualistic, and puts great stress on personal enlightenment. A cardinal feature of Protestant mysticism is the emphasis on the divine element in the human being, the spark, center, or ground of the soul, the divine image, and "inner light."

After the Reformation numerous groups of "spirituals" and mystically inclined Protestant individuals came into existence in Germany and Holland. In England the Cambridge Platonists and the Quakers greatly influenced mystical tendencies and devotions. The Protestant mystics rejected the Lutheran and Calvinist doctrine of the total corruption of human nature and explicitly recognized that the divine light or spark is a universal principle in all human beings. Thus George Fox appealed to the conscience of the American Indians as a proof of the universality of the "inner light," and William Law described non-Christian saints as "apostles of Christ within."

Protestant mystics stated plainly that the mystic's supreme authority lies not in the written word of scripture but in the Word of God himself. Dependence on external authority was replaced by the guiding light and freedom of inner experience and conscience. Not surprisingly, such an attitude was considered dangerously antinomian and brought many mystics into trouble with the Church authorities.

It is possible to gather a whole anthology of Protestant mystics from different Churches, countries and centuries. Three major figures from the seventeenth and eighteenth centuries are considered here. One of the most influential, though also most difficult, of the early Protestant mystics was the German Lutheran Jacob Boehme, who was in many ways a counterpart of the Rhenish mystics Eckhart, Tauler, and Suso.

Jacob Boehme (1575-1624)

The leading Lutheran representative of mystical piety, Jacob Boehme belongs to a strong current of radical dissent and heterodox, if not to say esoteric, mysticism which continues to exercize its influence to the present day. The son of a poor peasant family from a village in German Silesia, he was dreamy and introspective. With only a

An eighteenth-century engraving of Jacob Boehme. One of the best-known German Protestant mystics, his large corpus of highly speculative and controversial theosophical works inspired many other mystics, philosophers, painters, and writers.

his age between medieval and Renaissance thinking, expressing this through the dialectical principle that in "Yes and No, all things consist."

These ideas germinated in him for some years before he put them down on paper, writing at dawn before his work began. Thus his work *Aurora*, or *Dawn Glow*, came into being stage by stage, consisting of a mixture of theology, philosophy, astrology, and devotional texts. Unfortunately a copy of the manuscript fell into the hands of the town pastor, who denounced Boehme from his pulpit and threatened to have him arrested. The town magistrate asked him to leave but then agreed to let him stay, provided he handed over his manuscript and refrained from further writing.

Although Boehme complied, maintaining a long period of silence during which he read the "high masters," he became the center of a growing circle of admirers, kept up a wide correspondence and was active in a secret brotherhood. His learned friends introduced him to theosophical and alchemical writings, especially those of Paracelsus, the mystical physician, philosopher, and alchemist so deeply influenced by the teachings of the Kabbalah and Gnosticism. Boehme also read the *Sermons* of Tauler and the *Theologia Germanica*. After some years he decided to follow his own conscience and return to writing.

From 1619 until his death he poured forth a torrent of works of which the best known is *Mysterium Magnum,* a spiritual commentary on the book of Genesis. His various manuscripts circulated among his friends, but the only one published during his lifetime was *The Way to Christ,* which consists of several tracts on the mystical path, written in 1622. Boehme here

little education from the village school, he was apprenticed to a shoemaker and became entirely self-taught through his wide reading. His devotion to spiritual matters annoyed his master, who dismissed him, and Boehme began a long period of wandering as a traveling shoemaker, eventually settling in the town of Görlitz.

In 1600, newly married and a master shoemaker in his own right, he had a deep religious experience when he saw the origin of all things in a vision. Looking into a burnished pewter dish reflecting the sunshine, he fell into an inward ecstasy that made him "gaze into the very heart of things, the very herbs and grass, and…actual nature harmonized with what he had inwardly seen." This experience gave him a profound insight into resolving the tensions of

turns back from theosophical speculation to the traditions of German mysticism, although he intended no break with official Lutheranism. The work once again drew the wrath and invective of the town pastor: "There are as many blasphemies in this shoemaker's book as there are lines; it smells of shoemaker's pitch and filthy blacking." Boehme submitted to voluntary exile from the town and died soon afterwards.

One of the tracts of *The Way to Christ* consists of a dialog between a scholar and his master on how to see God and hear him speak. Here it is less a matter of the soul embracing Christ than of sinking oneself into the No-thing, the unconditioned *Ungrund,* out of which everything has come and to which everything will return. Human beings fell when they separated themselves from the All as ego-centered selves in a world of things and sensible images. If one wants to see and hear God, one must forsake this world of images and claim no things as one's own. Then one becomes a no-thing among no-things, and it is in this no-thingness that true love resides.

Boehme took the Gnostic belief that the physical world arose from a primeval fall which was repeated with the historic fall of Adam. Christ restores to the soul the divine reality lost to humankind through Adam's fall, and all things become renewed. The essential reality lies in an ideal world which Boehme describes as "the uncreated heaven." Thus heaven and hell are not places which human beings enter after death but represent present states of their souls.

The Four and Twenty Elders Casting their Crowns before the Divine Throne, by William Blake (c. 1803-5). This vision is described in Revelation 4. Blake's mystical and metaphysical works were influenced by Jacob Boehme's theosophy. (Tate Gallery, London)

An illustration from Boehme's *Alle Theosophische Werke,* published in Amsterdam in 1682. Boehme's mystical philosophy draws eclectically on sources from both inside and outside the Christian tradition. He combined apocalyptic and Gnostic ideas in his writings, which were condemned as heretical by the Church. (London Library)

Boehme's writings were published after his death and translated into English between 1647 and 1663. They are complex and difficult to understand, but in spite of their obscurities they exercized a profound influence on later intellectual movements and personalities, on

George Fox Preaching in a Tavern, by E. Wehnert, c.1850. Fox had experienced a deep inner transformation through his ardent love of God. He urged his followers to turn from darkness to the light of Christ within, a light present in every human being. (Popular print)

idealism and romanticism, on William Law and William Blake, on Schelling and Silesius, and many others.

Boehme's mystical philosophy is a strange synthesis of Lutheran theology, theosophy, and hermeticism. Parts of it are so impenetrable, yet so alluring, that any reader can feel both inspired and baffled. But there can be no doubt that the powerful mystical experiences of the simple shoemaker from Silesia continue to attract even in the twentieth century, when the Quaker Rufus Jones, the Protestant Paul Tillich, and the Orthodox Nicolas Berdyayev have all wrestled with Boehme's mysticism.

George Fox (1624-91)

Seventeenth-century England was rich in mystically minded men, in groups of spiritual seekers who renounced the outward forms of religion for a personal, inward quest, often influenced by Jacob Boehme's ideas. William Penn has said that these individuals "left all visible churches and societies and wandered up and down as sheep without a shepherd...*seeking* their Beloved, but could not find him as their souls desired to know him."

One such spiritual seeker was George Fox, whose religious genius initiated an important new movement, the Society of Friends, more generally known as Quakers, who for more than three hundred years have exerted considerable influence through their practice of religious and political toleration. Who was this deeply spiritual man and talented organizer who is one of the best-known Protestant mystics?

Fox was born into a pious Puritan weaver family living in Leicestershire, in England. His father had the reputation of a "Righteous Christer," and his mother was described as "of the stock of the martyrs." The young George developed "a gravity and stayedness of mind and spirit not usual in children." By the age of eleven he "knew pureness and righteousness" and acted faithfully "inwardly to God and outwardly to man." He was probably apprenticed to a cobbler for a while, and may also have tended sheep for some time. He received little formal education, but read widely, and there is no evidence of any adult business occupation, although he always seems to have had modest amounts of money at his disposal.

An engraved portrait of George Fox. As a youth, Fox underwent a profound conversion at a drinking party, when he heard the call to become a seeker of heavenly wisdom. This mystical experience set his life on a new path.

At the age of nineteen a drinking party with friends jolted him into a disturbing awareness in which he suddenly perceived a call "to forsake all, both young and old, and keep out of all, and be as a stranger to all." He now became a "seeker" in quest for "heavenly wisdom," and after three years of wandering to find spiritual assurance, he experienced an ecstatic revelation, a second birth, which gave him genuine mystical insight, later described in his spiritual autobiography, *The Journal of George Fox*. There he reports various religious experiences and direct revelations which he called "openings." These, in his view, corrected the traditional concepts of faith and practice in English life, especially the formalism and traditionalism of the established Church. They included the insight that the God who created heaven and earth does not dwell in temples and churches but in people's hearts, and also the affirmation that as women have souls just as men, they should be treated as equals. Once Fox had started his prophetic, peripatetic ministry, to which he devoted himself over the next forty years, it is not surprising that the first associate to join him in his work was a woman.

Fox placed the God-given inward light, found in every person, above creeds and scripture, so that true authority is founded on personal experience. This led to his critical, militant attitude towards ecclesiastical and social customs such as oaths, tithes, and military service. He had personally experienced that no priest could speak to his condition, his searching quest, but Christ himself, and he urged his followers to turn from darkness to the light of Christ within. Fox felt reassured that the love of God was always with him and he "was ravished with the sense of the love of God."

But he also knew that such love demands the renunciation of worldly comforts and desires: "It is the great love of God to make a wilderness of that which is pleasant to the outward eye and fleshly mind; and to make a fruitful field of barren wilderness." In one of his passages he describes how he came upon the Spirit, through the flaming sword, into God's paradise:

All things were new; and all the creation gave another smell unto me than before, beyond what words can utter. I knew nothing but pureness, innocency, and righteousness, being renewed up into the image of God by Christ Jesus; so that I was come up to the state of Adam, which he was in before he fell.

Fox experienced a profound personal and inward transformation which he believed could also transform all of England. As Jesus Christ had spoken to Fox's condition, so too could he speak to the condition of the whole country, for Christ came to end the old order and inaugurate a new.

Traveling on foot, George Fox started a vigorous prophetic ministry and was soon joined by itinerant men and women preachers, leading to the founding of local congregations. Fox had most success in gaining adherents in the Lake District and later in Yorkshire and London. He attracted a significant following, not only from the masses, but also from the elite, such as the cultured William Penn and Robert Barclay.

However, because Fox coupled his spiritual message with strong social protest, he created opposition and suffered public hostility, leading to repeated imprisonment. For example, he attacked the doffing of hats and discriminatory respect accorded to social class and station: "Oh,

Ruth Returning from Gleaning, by Samuel Palmer (1805-81). An admirer of William Blake, Palmer painted mystical pastoral landscapes that offer a vision of an idyllic rural England, a new Jerusalem. The figure of Ruth as pilgrim reflects the empowerment of women in this mystical radical vision. (Victoria & Albert Museum, London)

the rage and scorn, the heat and fury that arose! Oh, the blows, punchings, beatings, and imprisonments that we underwent for not putting off our hats to men!" He also opposed capital punishment and other practices. Many of his social views have a decidedly modern ring.

Later in life Fox traveled widely, visiting Ireland, the British colonies in the Caribbean and North America, especially Maryland and Rhode Island, and Holland and Germany. His health was damaged by the frequent beatings and imprisonments in dreadful conditions, and he suffered many illnesses towards the end of his life. He dictated his *Journal,* from which we can see that he was a strong, persistent, and courageous person with a gentle spirit. He always vigorously opposed nominal Christianity and preached that, to be a Christian, one must live like Christ in the world. He taught that there is a light within, open to all, wherein one can experience unity on earth. Salvation involves turning to this light, to Christ, which is both within and transcendent. Thus Fox stressed immediacy and realism in Christian experience. Christ is no figure of the past, about whom we read in a book or whose presence is found in sacramental forms, but is experienced in fellowship, in spiritual communion "which makes perfect." He said, "Christ is within thee, the hope of glory."

Fox's mystical spirituality and social concern live on through the Quakers who flourish on both sides of the Atlantic. Organized without any clergy, they maintain their continuing witness to the light within, "the light that lightens everyman," are prominent in pacifism and philanthropy, and have produced some fine spiritual teachers, among them the two Americans, John Woolman (1720-72), a campaigner against slavery who also had a Franciscan-like compassion for animals, and Thomas R. Kelly (1893-1941), whose *A Testament of Devotion* is an outstanding spiritual writing of the twentieth century.

William Law (1686-1761)

Another well-known Protestant mystic is the eighteenth-century Anglican divine William Law. He was born at King's Cliffe in Northamptonshire, in England. In 1705 he went as a student to Emmanuel College, Cambridge. Six years later the college made him a Fellow and at the same time he was ordained a deacon in the Anglican Church. In 1714, when King George I ascended the English throne, Law belonged to those who refused to pledge allegiance to the House of Hanover and consequently lost his fellowship. He then worked as a private tutor for some years, was fully ordained as a priest in 1727, and withdrew into retirement in 1740 to his native King's Cliffe. There he became the center of a small community and lived "the devout and holy life" to which he had exhorted others in his writings.

From the mid-1730s onward Law began to read extensively the works of Jacob Boehme, "that wonderful man," as he called him. He became Boehme's greatest English disciple, but is best remembered for his own book, *A Serious Call to a Devout and Holy Life* (1728), which inspired John and Charles Wesley's "Holy Club" in Oxford, where they developed their main ideas for the evangelical revival of England. John Wesley said of the book that it "will hardly be excelled, if it be equalled, in the English tongue, either for the beauty of expression or for justice and depth of thought." The book also influenced Samuel Johnson, and stimulated an interest in religion in him.

Earlier, Law had published *A Practical Treatise Upon Christian Perfection* (1726), but it was especially in his second book that he set out tight, rational arguments for a "devout and holy life" in order to defend Christian faith and practice against the challenge of the Age of Reason. Law considered *A Serious Call to a Devout and Holy Life* his best work, for its shows that the Christian ideal for human life is actualized through a disciplined practice of personal mysticism.

Law later wrote several other treatises stressing the union between creator and creature, such as *The Spirit of Prayer* (1749) and *The Spirit of Love* (1752). These are more mystical in character and are inspired by Dionysius, Ruusbroec, Tauler, and Suso, but most of all Boehme. In Law's view, the eternal Word is lying hidden within all human beings. It is a spark of the divine nature which gives the soul a depth, center, and infinity which he calls the hidden "pearl of eternity."

Like Boehme, Law stresses the primacy of the will. When the human will turns to itself, it breaks off from divine harmony and falls into misery. Self is the root, tree, and branches of all evil; to live the life of self is to live in separation from God. When the will is rightly applied in prayer, it can be effective in creating new life, for "the prayer of the heart, the prayer of faith, has a kindling and creating power, and forms and transforms the soul into everything that its desires reach after: it…brings us into real union and communion with God."

Law makes it clear that devotion entails the dedication of one's whole life to God, not just a part of it. It is the full living out of one's commitment to God in *all* of life, so that prayer is only "the smallest part" of devotion. But unless the lives of individuals match their prayers, the latter are only "lip labor" at best and pure hypocrisy at worst. Law also maintained that persons of leisure hold a special responsibility to devote themselves to God in a higher degree than others, living for God "at all times" and "in all places." This duty includes the responsible use of one's time, one's estate, and one's fortune. The freer a person is from the pursuit of the basic necessities of life, the more he should "imitate the higher perfections of angels."

William Law has been described as one of the most profound English religious writers. On reading Boehme's works, he was converted from a narrow Christianity to a wide, philosophic mysticism. His influential writings burn with mystic passion, while his interpretation of Boehme ensured that the inspired shoemaker's mighty vision of the human being and the universe found an abiding place in English literature.

The Angel Standing in the Sun, by J.M.W. Turner (1775-1851). This powerful atmospheric painting links the artist's heightened perception of reality with the inner vision of the mystic. For those with eyes to see, the world is filled with the glory of God. (The Tate Gallery, London)

CHAPTER FIVE

EASTERN ORTHODOX MYSTICS

The Eastern Orthodox Churches possess a mystical heritage of great splendor, a heritage that was passed from Byzantium to the Eastern Orthodox Churches in Greece, Russia, Bulgaria, and elsewhere in the East. The foundations of the Orthodox mystical tradition are the same as for Western Christianity: the early Church Fathers, the Bible, and Greek thought. But soon mystical writers in East and West differed in their understanding of the different stages of the mystical way, the nature of mystical union, and the presence of God in the world.

The Greek Father Evagrius of Pontus (346-99) distinguished between three stages in the spiritual journey to God. The first was the active life, freed from passions and characterized by purity of heart; the second was natural contemplation, which sees God in all things and all things in God; the third, called *theoria,* was the contemplation of God face to face, in an unmediated union of love.

Gregory of Nyssa (330-95), in his *Life of Moses*, spoke of three somewhat different stages, each corresponding to a manifestation of God to Moses in Exodus: as *light* (the burning bush), *cloud* (the pillar of cloud and fire) and *darkness* (on the summit of Mount Sinai). This corresponds to the three Dionysian stages of purification, illumination, and union. While these stages were widely accepted in the West, the Christian East more commonly followed the pattern established by Evagrius.

He described the *nous*—the mind in its direct understanding of spiritual truth through intuition—as that faculty whereby human beings apprehend God in contemplative prayer. Other writers, however, looked to the heart as the spiritual center where each person is most authentically "in the image of God." Later, during the fourteenth century, these two approaches of emphasizing either the mind or the heart were combined in "the prayer of the *nous* in the heart."

Athanasius of Alexandria, in the fourth

The monastery of Optina Pystin, on the Zhizdra river, Russia. The richness of Orthodox mystical spirituality is reflected in the beauty of its ancient monasteries and churches.

Icon of the Trinity, by Andrei Rublyev (c. 1360-1430). This famous icon represents what the Orthodox call "the Old Testament Trinity." God visited Abraham under the oaks of Mamre in the form of three men, to whom Abraham offered hospitality (Gen. 18). Christian theologians interpreted this event as a prefiguration of the Trinity. (Tretyakov Gallery, Moscow)

century, had summed up the message of salvation in Christ in the sentence: "He became man that we might be made God." In other words, God became "incarnate" in humankind so that human beings might be "ingodded." The Eastern Orthodox tradition has reflected on both parts of this statement. From the fourth to the seventh centuries Greek theologians discussed primarily what it meant for God to become human, for Jesus to be fully God and truly human in one single, undivided person. In the centuries that followed attention shifted to the second part of Athanasius's statement "...that we might be made God." How can the human being, without ceasing to be authentically human, enjoy union with God in His glory? What is meant by the process of deification or "ingodding" (*theosis*), and how can it be achieved?

Central to the process of transformation leading to union with God is the ascent to God through contemplative prayer. No particular technique is considered as privileged in achieving the necessary inner stillness (*hesychia*), in order to progress from the discursive thinking of the mind to that of non-discursive, unmediated union. The Christian East has developed the so-called "Jesus prayer," a short and frequently repeated invocation to Jesus, mostly in the form "Lord Jesus Christ, Son of God, have mercy on

Illumination of Gregory of Nazianzus, c. 1100. He and his contemporaries Basil the Great and Gregory of Nyssa, the "Cappadocian Fathers," deeply influenced Orthodox theology and mysticism. (Bodleian Library, Oxford)

me." This may be formally recited at prayer time in church or at home, or it can just be repeated during the day whilst going about one's normal activities.

This important prayer, with widely varying formulations, is sometimes called a "Christian mantra." But this is misleading, because the Jesus prayer is not simply a rhythmic incantation but implies belief in the Incarnation and is addressed to Jesus as Son of God. The repetition of the Jesus prayer concentrates the mind on the presence of God leading to an ecstatic vision of the divine light, penetrating the soul through the divine energy implicit in the name of Jesus.

Eastern Orthodox mystics distinguish between the essence of God and his attributes or energies which penetrate the universe. The whole of creation is a process of divine emanation whereby God's being is transported outside himself "to dwell in the heart of all things." Fundamental to Orthodox mysticism is the divinization of the human being which comes about through contemplative prayer, fostered especially through the method of *hesychasm*, developed by Symeon the New Theologian in the eleventh century, and through the Jesus prayer. Many people in the West first became familiar with the Jesus prayer through *The Way of the Pilgrim,* a nineteenth-century account by a Russian layman which became very popular then, but this prayer has more ancient roots. It became known first during the fourteenth century, and was further promoted in the eighteenth century by the *Philokalia*, a rich collection of spiritual texts. Its translation led to a much greater knowledge of the Jesus prayer in Russia and Romania. Following the renewed interest in the Orthodox tradition during the late twentieth century in the West, the Jesus prayer is now also practiced by many Western Christians. Modern Orthodox writers describe it as a prayer that begins as *prayer of the lips*, recited aloud, which gradually grows more interior and thus becomes a *prayer of the intellect* or mind (*nous*), which in turn is transformed into a *prayer of the heart.*

The Orthodox mystical tradition possesses a great richness of themes and personalities. Many different mystics and mystically oriented groups are known from Eastern countries, especially from Russia. Eastern mystics were often rigidly ascetic, yet at the same time laid great stress on the transforming power of love which is itself divine. It is through this power that human nature is perfected and united with God. From the great richness of the Eastern tradition, only a few seminal figures and their key ideas can be considered here.

The writings of Gregory of Nyssa and Dionysius were of considerable influence for the development of Orthodox mysticism, but by far the most towering figure of the Byzantine tradition is that of Maximus the Confessor, whose thought embodies some of the best insights of the Eastern tradition and represents the full flowering of Greek Christian thought. His greatest contribution lies in developing further the ideas first explored by Gregory and

Dionysius that the whole world is penetrated and shaped by the *energeia,* the activity of God, whereas God himself remains hidden, unknown and incomprehensible to human minds. Yet unity with God can be found through love.

Maximus the Confessor (c. 580-662)

Maximus was born into an aristocratic Christian family in Constantinople, now the modern city of Istanbul. Probably a well-educated man, he worked for several years as court secretary to the East Roman Emperor Heraclius I, before becoming a monk in 613 in the monastery of Chrysopolis. The Persian invasion in 626 caused him to flee to North Africa, where he took part in vigorous controversies about the nature of Christ. Called to Rome, he became involved in intricate theological-political disputes which eventually, in 653, led the emperor to have him arrested along with the pope.

He was tried for treason and tortured by having his tongue cut out and his right hand cut off for refusing to stop preaching against Monotheletism, the doctrine that Christ has only one, divine will. He died shortly thereafter near the Black Sea and soon received the name "Confessor" because of the boldness of his attitude towards the emperor.

Maximus transmitted the ideas of Dionysius the Areopagite to the Eastern Church. His commentaries on the Greek Fathers considerably influenced the theology of the Middle Ages. An independent, original thinker, Maximus was a great speculative theologian who left approximately ninety major works, including *Commentary on the "Our Father"* and *The Four*

Icon of Christ the Redeemer. The great cosmological and anthropological speculations of Maximus the Confessor always centered on Christ, who is the principal link between God and his creation. (Museum of Macedonia, Skopje)

A twelfth-century icon of the Last Judgment, from St. Catherine's Monastery, Sinai. This unusual painting shows people ascending a ladder toward God in heaven, from which the sinners fall down into hell. Inspired by a treatise by John Climacus, the ladder was a metaphor for moral aspiration.

Hundred Chapters on Love, which describe how human beings can achieve union with God.

These chapters, or brief paragraphs, integrate the desire for meditation with an empathy for human affairs and active charity. Most crucial is love for the knowledge *of* God, not just a knowledge *about* God. Maximus warns that it "is impossible to reach the habit of this love if one has any attachment to earthly things." There exists a reciprocal relationship between love and detachment: as detachment gives rise to love, so deepest love for God causes the mind to become completely detached from all things. Love for others is a key element in the contemplative life as it is a measure of one's purity. The pure mind is illumined by divine light, and the pure person is free from attachment to all objects of desire.

Maximus says that no one knows why God created when he did, for God's wisdom is not subject to human knowledge. Together with most other mystics, he affirms that God is both knowable and unknowable: knowable in ideas about him, but unknowable in himself. Experience of and participation in God are the way to know God.

The originality of Maximus's thought is apparent in his great cosmological and anthropological speculations. His greatest contribution lies in developing further the idea,

A ninth-century illustration of St. Catherine's monastery at the foot of Mount Sinai, with Climacus in a cave in the background. (Princeton University Library, N.J.)

found in both Gregory of Nyssa and Dionysius, that the human being is a mediator between God and the cosmos. This includes his teaching on the "deification" or restoration of created humanity in God through Christ and the Holy Spirit. His thought is Christocentric, culminating in his vision of the Incarnation as the goal of history. Christ is the central principle between God and his creation. When a human being gives himself entirely to God's love and is united with him by grace, he penetrates entirely into God and becomes God, without losing his identity of being human. It is in Christ that God has become man and man has become God. This union of God and the human being in Christ is realized again and again in human experience through ecstatic love, through mystical union.

This union is a mutual participation in the qualities and mode of existence of each other, a mutual *perichoresis,* or interpenetration, which unites God and the human being without destroying their identity. This penetration takes place on behalf of the whole of creation, thereby bridging the chasm between creator and creation through an act of mutual love, sustained by God's grace and the freely responding human will. In effect, both God and the human being go out of themselves to reach towards the other finding union in love.

The ideas of Maximus present a balance of spiritual theory and practice not always achieved by subsequent theologians. His work marks the end of the so-called patristic period. In the opinion of a contemporary Orthodox writer, little progress has been made in the Eastern tradition since Maximus the Confessor: "There is the scholastic systematization of patristic thought in John of Damascus, its ascetical working out in Gregory of Palamas, its liturgical interpretation in Nicolas Cabasilas, but none of this attains the grandeur of conception characteristic of Gregory, Dionysius, and Maximus."

Great influence on Christian monasticism in the East was exercised by an almost contemporary of Maximus, the ascetic **John Climacus** (579-649), who was first a monk and later abbot of the monastery of St. Catherine on Mount Sinai. He was called "Climacus" because of his famous work *The Ladder of Divine Ascent,* or "Ladder of Paradise" (*klimax,* meaning "ladder" in Greek). Using the biblical image of Jacob's ladder reaching up to heaven, with angels ascending and descending, he describes the ascent to God in thirty steps to correspond with the ages of Christ at the time of his baptism. Another shorter treatise, *To the Shepherd,* describes the task of the abbot or spiritual father. *The Ladder of Divine Ascent* is read in Orthodox monasteries during Lent and the famous ladder is frequently depicted in icons and manuscripts. It shows the spiritual father ushering the monks to the foot of the ladder, with good angels assisting them to ascend while evil angels are trying to pull them off, dropping them into the gaping jaws of hell.

After the influential figures of Maximus the Confessor and John Climacus of the seventh century, the next Orthodox mystic of lasting influence is Symeon the New Theologian.

Symeon the New Theologian (949-1032)

Born into a noble family in Asia Minor the young George, as was his original name, was sent at the age of eleven to the imperial capital of Constantinople for his education. Reared by an uncle there, he was destined for a political career. At fourteen he placed himself under the spiritual direction of the monk Symeon the Pious, at the monastery of Studios, while continuing the preparation for his political career. At the age of about twenty, when praying one night, he had a powerful inner experience, receiving the first of a series of visions of divine light. He eventually became an imperial senator, but at the age of twenty-seven he decided to enter the monastery of Studios, placing himself entirely under the direction of his spiritual father, whose name he adopted. The close relationship between the two Symeons became such a source of concern for the abbot that he soon asked the young Symeon to choose between going to another monastery or ceasing to have the older man as spiritual father.

It was thus that the young Symeon joined the monastery of St. Mamas in Constantinople, where he was ordained a priest and then elected as abbot, an office he held for a quarter of a century. He revitalized the prayer life of this monastery and soon transformed it into a model community. Eventually, however, he got into trouble over his spiritual methods, and especially for his devotion to Symeon the Pious, whom he began to venerate immediately after his death. The ecclesiastical authorities forced him to resign as abbot and later exiled him to a small hermitage on the opposite shore of the Bosphorus. Living there at the ruined church of St. Marina, he soon transformed it into a thriving monastery, and also continued the writing he had begun at St. Mamas. Eventually Symeon was rehabilitated and offered a bishopric, but he preferred to spend his remaining years at St. Marina, where he died in 1032.

Formed within the social and political context of the late Byzantine empire, Symeon's thought is deeply rooted in the rich tradition of the Eastern Christian writers who preceded him. Like them, he describes the power of contemplative prayer in developing the ability to see God in all of creation and ultimately to behold God in himself. Symeon added significantly to this tradition, and also modified it. Like other writers before him, he insisted upon the divine mystery and the apophatic approach to God. But God is not only the transcendent Other. He can be known here and now, in this present life, through direct personal experience, not only by monks but also by lay people. Symeon insisted that one "who has wife and children, crowds of servants, much property, and a prominent position in the world" can yet attain the vision of God, for it is possible to live "a heavenly life here on earth...not just in caves or mountains or monastic cells, but in the midst of cities."

Unlike Dionysius's "dazzling darkness," Symeon preferred to use the symbolism of light in speaking about the mystical union with God, which takes the form of a vision of divine radiance. Thus the preferred biblical model is not Moses's experience at Sinai, but Christ's transfiguration on Mount Tabor. "We bear witness that God is light, and that those counted worthy to see him have all beheld him as light, and those who have received him have received him as light, for the light of his glory goes before him."

Symeon's spiritual doctrine is rooted in the tradition of Evagrius, John Climacus, and Maximus the Confessor. His writings consist of doctrinal and moral instructions called *catecheses*, sermons preached to his monks, a series of short rules, and above all his fifty-six *Hymns of Divine Love*, which describe his spiritual experiences. Symeon is exceptional among Greek theologians in referring explicitly to his own personal experience, for the Christian East knows of no equivalent to Augustine's autobiographical *Confessions*.

The *Hymns of Divine Love* are powerful poems celebrating the contemplation of God as a vision and experience of indwelling, as a "light and fire" which ultimately are the gift of divine outpouring rather than the result of sustained mental prayer. His first vision seems to suggest that the light is impersonal, but elsewhere Christ speaks to him from within the light, and the vision leads to a dialogue of love between them. Symeon's vision of light is a direct, unmediated union with God. It affirms that human beings can participate not only in the energies but in the very essence of God: "O light that none can name, for it is altogether nameless, O light with many names, for it is at work in all things..." It is also a vision which is deeply sacramental when he writes about the eucharist, the Christian sacrament of communion with the body and blood of Christ, in strongly realist terms:

John the Theologian of Patmos, a late fifteenth-century icon from the Trinity-Sergiev Monastery. (Private Collection)

My blood has been mingled with your Blood,
And I know that I have been united also to your
Godhead.
I have become your most pure Body;
A member dazzling, a member truly sanctified,
A member glorious, transparent, luminous;...
What was I once, what have I now become!...

Symeon, more than any other author, sets the divine light at the center of his spiritual teaching, although God remains always a mystery beyond all understanding, "invisible, unapproachable, beyond...our grasp." Yet at the same time God has become truly human and can be known in a vision face to face. Symeon's work explores the love of God for human beings in some of the most poetic hymns of all mystical literature, hymns of joyful praise to God, celebrating the deep spiritual intimacy and union of the whole person, body and soul together, with its divine source and creator.

Symeon was called "the New Theologian" to mark him from two earlier figures held in great Christian esteem—John the Evangelist, or the Divine, known as "the Theologian" in Greek, and the fourth-century Gregory of Nazianzus, referred to as "Gregory the Theologian" in the Christian East. Both men celebrated the splendor of mystical prayer, and since Symeon renewed this tradition in the eleventh century, he was given the title "Symeon the *New* Theologian." His mystical theology became a formative influence on hesychasm, the tradition of mystical prayer practiced in the Orthodox Church, especially at Mount Athos, and also on the Jesus prayer, although Symeon himself never referred to this directly. Hesychasm came to its full flowering in the fourteenth century with Gregory of Palmas.

St. Gregory of Palamas (1296–1359)

Like Symeon and others before him, Gregory compared God to light rather than darkness, and drew on solar, not nocturnal symbolism. His model of mystical union was not Moses ascending Mount Sinai to find God in "thick darkness," but Moses's vision of the "pavement of sapphire stone" and the "firmament of heaven in its clarity," and Ezekiel's vision of a chariot of fire and Christ's transfiguration in resplendent light.

Probably born in Constantinople, into a distinguished family connected with the imperial court, Gregory was educated in the classical philosophies of antiquity and called to a political career. However, attracted to monastic life from an early age, he decided after the death of his father to renounce imperial service and become a monk. He also persuaded his mother, brothers and sisters to follow his example of embracing the religious life.

In 1318 Gregory went with his two brothers to Mount Athos in north-eastern Greece, which had by then become a spiritual stronghold and influential center of Greek Orthodoxy. The monasteries of Mount Athos were not the oldest ones of the Christian East, for other mountain monasteries existed earlier elsewhere. The main monastery of Mount Athos was founded only in the tenth century but, with the Turkish invasion of Asia Minor, it acquired unique importance, further enhanced by the multi-national composition of its monks, drawn from Greece, Serbia, Bulgaria, Georgia and Russia. Until the fourteenth century even a Latin monastery of the Western Church existed on Mount Athos, supported by monks from Italy.

Once on Mount Athos, Gregory studied and reflected on the writings of earlier Greek theologians for many years. Under the guidance of a spiritual father he became a master of the contemplative life and in turn guided other monks on the path of hesychasm, or the prayer of the quiet.

Soon Turkish raids forced him to interrupt his monastic life and flee to Thessalonica, where he was ordained a priest in 1326. Subsequently he retired with ten companions to a hermitage in Macedonia, but returned to Athos in 1331 and soon became engaged in the hesychast controversy between Greek and Latin scholastic theologians. It was particularly Barlaam the Calabrian, a Greek monk residing in Italy, who tried to discredit the contemplative practices of the hesychasts.

Hesychasm is a Byzantine contemplative and ascetical movement which integrates repetitive prayer formulas, especially the Jesus prayer, with bodily postures and controlled breathing in order to reach a state of deep inner peace and mystical union. Its origins go back to the early Greek fathers, but its full practice was developed by figures such as Gregory of Sinai, Nicephorus of Mount Athos, and above all Gregory of Palamas.

The praying person is seated rather than standing, as was the custom in the East, and is advised to have the head bowed down, "resting your beard on your chest and directing your bodily eye together with your entire intellect towards the middle of your belly, that is, toward your navel." Other texts suggest that the gaze is to be fixed on the heart, the deep center, where the human being finds unity. Breathing should be carefully controlled in rhythm with the Jesus prayer and, according to modern sources, the prayer may also be co-ordinated with the beating of the heart itself. Thus the intellect or *nous* can dispel all thoughts and search inwardly the true place of the heart where inner simplicity, free from all images and discursive thinking, is reached.

These physical techniques bear a striking similarity to those of yoga and Sufism which also involve the control of breathing and the concentration of attention upon specific psycho-somatic centers of the human body. It is possible, though unclear, that the Byzantine hesychasts may have been influenced by Sufi masters. It is certain, however, that the development of hesychasm helped Eastern Christianity to survive almost four hundred years of Muslim occupation after the fall of Constantinople in 1453. With its simple character and precepts, hesychast spirituality inspired monks and lay people alike, and could simply be handed down without schools, literature, or clerical leadership, through the practice of its techniques and prayers, even when Orthodox spirituality no longer enjoyed official support.

According to Gregory of Palamas, the prayer of the heart leads eventually to the vision of the divine light which even in this present life can be seen with the eyes of the body. This light is identical with the radiant splendor which surrounded Jesus at his Transfiguration on Mount Tabor, for it is none other than the uncreated energies of the Godhead. Palamas distinguished specifically between the essence of God, which remains unknowable, and his divine energies, which permeate all things and can be directly experienced by the human being in the form of deifying grace.

Icon of St. Gregory of Palamas, nineteenth century. This medieval theologian is one of the most influential mystics of the Orthodox Church. He developed a mysticism of light rather than darkness in speaking about his encounter with God. (Private Collection)

His opponent, Barlaam, argued differently, however, by maintaining God's unknowability in an extreme form and taking a contrary view on the possibility of attaining a divine vision here and now. He also attacked the importance of using the body in prayer and caricatured the hesychasts as "those men who locate the soul in their navel" (*omphalopsychoi*).

It was in answer to his criticisms that Gregory wrote his chief work, *Triads in Defence of the Holy Hesychasts.* Rooted in the biblical vision of the unity of the human being, body and soul together, he fused Platonic and Aristotelian ideas to express his spiritual experience and provide a solid theological foundation for Orthodox mystical theology transmitted through hesychast practice. He argued that the physical exercises used by the hesychasts in prayer, and their claim to see the divine light with their bodily eyes, could be defended as wholly legitimate. His opponents accused him of heresy, but his views were vindicated by several councils. His defense of mystical prayer and practice set a definitive standard for centuries to come and profoundly influenced the shape of Orthodox spirituality.

In 1347 Gregory was elected bishop of Thessalonica, but because of unstable political conditions could not take possession of his see before 1350. In 1354, during a journey to Constantinople, he was captured by the Turks and held in captivity for a year, after which he returned to Thessalonica, where he died in 1359. In 1368, nine years after his death, he was proclaimed a saint and his great importance was recognized by calling him "Father and Doctor of the Orthodox Church."

According to Palamas's near contemporary, the Cypriot monk **Gregory of Sinai** (d.1346), who also lived on Mount Athos, the vision of divine light has a profoundly transforming effect upon the visionary by transporting him into the glory he contemplates, so that he himself becomes surrounded by dazzling light. Transported in ecstasy "to the non-material realm of inconceivable divine light," the intellect of the aspirant is "kindled into flame by the fire of the Godhead, and it is dissolved in its thoughts and swallowed up by the divine light, becoming itself entirely divine light of surpassing radiance." Just as Christian mystics in the West have often physically entered into the mystery of the cross and received the *stigmata*, the signs of Christ's physical wounds—a phenomenon completely unknown in the Christian East—so Eastern Orthodox mystics have entered the mystery of Christ's transfiguration in their bodily experience and been taken up into God's uncreated splendor, thereby experiencing glorification of the body in anticipation of its future glory, a foretaste of eternal life to come.

Such a view is based not on Platonist dualism, where the soul is trapped in the body as in a prison, but on a holistic biblical vision of the human being as an integral whole of mind and matter, where the body shares with the soul in the experience of the divine light and is deified along with the soul. This is the full effect of the Incarnation, of God made man in Christ. The modern Orthodox theologian Vladimir Lossky has defined this divine light or effulgence as

> ...the visible quality of the divinity, of the energies or grace in which God makes Himself known...This light is a light which fills at the same time both intellect and senses, revealing

itself to the whole man, and not only to one of his faculties. The divine light, being given in mystical experience, surpasses at the same time both sense and intellect.

Hesychast spirituality speaks to all, monks and lay people alike, and though developed in the past, it can still be followed today. It is a universal path which has been handed down from the Middle Ages to the modern world. When Gregory of Sinai left Mount Athos in 1335, he spent the last years of his life on the borders between the Byzantine Empire and Bulgaria, his teachings thus forming an important link between the Greek and Slav world of Orthodoxy. His disciples were instrumental in spreading the practice of hesychasm throughout Bulgaria, Serbia and Russia. It is in these countries that hesychast prayer practices enjoyed a great renaissance during the eighteenth and nineteenth centuries, especially through the publication of the *Philokalia* and *The Way of the Pilgrim*.

Philokalia (1782) and *The Way of the Pilgrim* (1884)

Created a century apart, these two books have exercized an enormous influence in making Orthodox mysticism and spirituality known to the modern world. During Turkish rule following the fall of Constantinople in the mid-fifteenth century, the life of the Greek Orthodox Church was marked by rigid traditionalism and a defensive stance toward its patristic heritage. But during the second part of the eighteenth century a hesychast renaissance occurred which led to the publication of the *Philokalia,* considered a *summa* of Byzantine spirituality which integrates into one vision the writings of the Fathers, the monastic doctrine and experience of prayer, and the ascetical way of life.

The title *Philokalia* is taken from the early Church Fathers. It was first given to an anthology of Origen's writings in the fourth century, and means "love of the beautiful," about that beauty which is more than simply an alternative to the "wisdom of the world." In a Platonic and Neoplatonic context, Beauty coincides with the highest Good. It is an invisible and uncreated Presence, in which the Light of Truth is united with divine love in a marriage which gives birth to that inner peace and stillness denoted by the word *hesychia.* Several smaller anthologies of hesychast prayer were collected over the centuries, but it was the *Philokalia,* compiled in the late eighteenth century by Macarius of Corinth and Nicodemus of the Holy Mountain (Mount Athos) and first published in Venice in 1782, which became a modern Orthodox classic.

The *Philokalia* is an anthology of Orthodox ascetical and mystical writings from the fourth to the fifteenth centuries, dealing with teachings on hesychasm and the Jesus prayer. It is a manual, guide and companion to the hesychast prayer of the heart and contains extracts from Evagrius, Maximus the Confessor, Symeon the New Theologian, Nicephorus the Hesychast, Gregory of Sinai, Gregory of Palamas and others, but nothing from the Cappadocian fathers or Dionysius the Areopagite. The bringing together of these texts into one volume adds potency to each and increases their mutual influence. The inner purpose of the spiritual way is stressed,

involving sobriety, attentiveness, stillness, and continuing remembrance of God. The invocation of the name of Jesus is recommended as unceasing prayer, and this Jesus prayer helps to unite the intellect and heart to achieve a state of communion with God, free from all concepts and images.

Although these texts were originally written by and addressed to monks, their eighteenth-century editors intended them for all Christians. Following the Orthodox tradition, the *Philokalia* strongly recommends personal direction by a spiritual father and emphasizes close links between spirituality and theology. This anthology of spiritual writings soon exercised a wide influence. By 1793 it was translated into Slavonic, and a Russian version appeared in the late nineteenth century. During the twentieth century numerous translations into Western languages were made, although the full translation into English has not yet been completed. A partial translation from the Russian version is available as *Writings from the Philokalia on the Prayer of the Heart.*

In Russia the *Philokalia* revived the earlier Russian hesychast tradition of the fifteenth century and also encouraged spiritual direction under the guidance of an elder, called *staretz.* One such elder has achieved immortal fame far beyond the boundaries of Orthodoxy through the figure of Zosima, described in Dostoevsky's novel *The Brothers Karamazov.*

No other spiritual counselor or *staretz* gained as much following as the anonymous pilgrim who wrote "The sincere accounts of a pilgrim to his spiritual father," known in English as *The Way of the Pilgrim* and published in Russia in 1884. The pilgrim was an avid reader of the *Philokalia.* It was St. Paul's phrase "pray without ceasing" which first sent this pilgrim on his search for the prayer of the heart.

The Way of the Pilgrim shows how hesychast spirituality could find devoted practitioners far beyond monastery walls. The account is perhaps originally the work of a simple peasant giving us a glimpse of the extended pilgrimages formerly undertaken by members of the Russian peasant community.

The book, a classic of Russian Orthodox spirituality, has been called "a sophisticatedly unsophisticated work," and is written with passionate intensity. The anonymous author describes himself as a pilgrim, traveling from place to place in Russia and Siberia. He learned the Jesus prayer from a master who also taught him to read the *Philokalia* with the eyes of the spirit. Arranged in a series of narratives, the book tells the story of the pilgrim's learning, practicing, and on occasion teaching to others, the hesychast way of praying. The ultimate aim of praying is to realize the human vocation of union with God so that eventually the pilgrim experiences the whole world as transfigured:

The prayer of the heart provided me with such delight, that I doubted if there were anyone happier than I on earth, or if there could be greater and finer delight in the very kingdom of heaven. Not only did I feel this in my innermost soul, but also all that was around me appeared to me in a delightful form, and all prompted me to love God and to thank him, people, trees, plants, animals, everything was akin to me, on all I found the impress of the name of Jesus Christ.

Perhaps no other book has inspired people more than *The Way of the Pilgrim* to discover Orthodox spirituality and learn the practice of the Jesus prayer. But beside the influence of this work, a powerful witness to the renewed vitality of Orthodox spirituality, there is also the continuing ministry of spiritual direction or eldership within Orthodoxy, a ministry not only exercized by monks, but at times equally by nuns who act as spiritual mothers, and in a more indirect way, by individual spiritual figures who present new mystic insights, as did the nineteenth-century Russian philosopher and poet Vladimir Solovyov.

Vladimir Solovyov (1853-1900)

Solovyov is a truly modern figure, highly complex, subtle and unusually wide-ranging in his intellectual and existential orientation, yet a faithful son of the Orthodox Church, someone who belongs to the great tradition of Russian "God-seekers." A mystic, poet, prophet, and philosopher who understood philosophy in its original sense as the search for wisdom, he commanded wide authority through his rigorously scholarly works, whereas his relentless striving for harmonious unity has encouraged others to explore a similar path. His theological ideas are as inspiring as they are contentious, and not without reason has Solovyov been called a "Russian Newman."

Son of the eminent historian Sergey Solovyov, the young Vladimir received his first education in languages, history, and philosophy in his Orthodox home, where he grew up as one of twelve children. His mother, who was related to an earlier religious philosopher, probably had a considerable influence on his development. Vladimir's religious feelings as a child were intense. He received the first of three formative mystical visions during a church service in 1862, when he was just nine years old.

Later, when he studied at Moscow University, the strength of his religious convictions gave way to an equally intense commitment to nihilistic and materialistic creeds. As a precocious and unusually hard-working student, he first took up natural sciences and then philosophy. He soon became tired of a merely critical, intellectual approach and looked for "positive content." It was then that he discovered Spinoza and Western mystics such as Boehme and others. Eventually he decided to attend the Moscow Theological Academy and read extensively in patristic theology. At the age of twenty-one he defended a highly acclaimed thesis on *The Crisis of Western Philosophy* and, as a result, was offered a lectureship in philosophy at the University of Moscow.

Soon afterwards, in 1875, he applied for study leave to go to England. He worked at the British Museum, reading Kabbalistic and other mystical literature, and it was in the Museum's Reading Room that he experienced his second mystical vision. He prayed to Sophia, the feminine embodiment of Divine Wisdom, asking her to reveal herself to him as she had done in his childhood. He saw only her face, but she commanded him to go to Egypt to find a fuller vision there, which he did.

Although little is known about his travels, he spent November 1875 to March 1876 in Egypt, where he was granted another vision, this time in the Sahara desert. He experienced there such a profound sense of universal harmony that it influenced his entire religious philosophy and gave him a sense of deep inner peace and oneness, which he tried to convey in some of his poems:

> *What is, what has been, what is yet to come,*
> *My unmoving gaze embraced all this...*
> *Below me seas and rivers appear blue,*
> *And the distant forest also, and snow-capped*
>   *mountains.*
>
> *I saw everything, everything was just one,*
> *Just one image of feminine beauty...*

And again:

> *Barriers are sundered, fetters are melted*
> *By the divine fire,*
> *And the eternal dawn of a new life rises*
> *In all, and all in One.*

This photograph, dating from 1887, conveys something of the intense and passionate nature of the young Vladimir Solovyov.

Sophia, the feminine embodiment of wisdom, represented as a winged figure on a throne. The Holy Wisdom provides an important feminine presence and motif in Christian mystical theology, and is especially highly regarded by Orthodox Christians. Russian icon of the Moscow School, seventeenth century. (Mark Gallery, London)

After traveling through different parts of Europe, Solovyov returned to Russia and resumed his lecturing. Between 1877 and 1881 he delivered his celebrated *Lectures on God-manhood*. He argued that the unique intermediary between the world and God can only be the human being, who alone is that vital part of nature capable of knowing and expressing the divine idea. The perfect revelation of God is Christ's Incarnation in human nature; his theandric (God-man) action integrates human history with God and has initiated a process of human transformation into Christ.

During the same period of 1877-81 he also developed a close friendship with Dostoevsky, accompanying him on his visit to the *staretz* Amvrosy in the monastery of Optina, the model for Dostoevsky's Father Zosima. It has been suggested that Solovyov himself was the inspiration for certain traits in the character of one or the other of the brothers Karamazov.

In 1880, while working on two important philosophical books, Solovyov also submitted a doctoral thesis to the University of St. Petersburg and was subsequently appointed a lecturer. However, the lectureship soon came to an end because he argued publicly that the new Tsar, Alexander III, as a Christian monarch, should show clemency towards the men who assassinated his father in March 1881. From then until the end of his life, Solovyov earned his livelihood from his writing alone. It was a period of intense activity and great loneliness. Questions of Russian history, culture, and theology much preoccupied him, but so did his great vision of a synthesis of religion, philosophy, science, and ethics in the context of universal Christianity. Solovyov was an early advocate of

the reunion of the Orthodox and Roman Catholic Churches, as he could see no substantial reasons for their continued separation. But this did not endear him to some of his compatriots. For a long time he was forbidden to publish articles on theology, and he did not lecture publicly for many years.

In 1898 he traveled once more through Europe and briefly revisited Egypt, but most of the time moved between Moscow and St. Petersburg, spending the summer with friends. He was truly a "wandering pilgrim," someone "with no fixed home or roots in this earthly word, a man whose sights and energies were wholly directed to the world of the spirit." A homeless wanderer, he was overcome by illness in his forty-eighth year and said when dying, "The Lord's work is difficult."

Besides his *Lectures on Godmanhood* there are other works which present his spiritual philosophy, especially *The Spiritual Foundations of Life,* translated into English as *God, Man and the Church,* and *The Meaning of Love.* Solovyov was consumed by the spiritual ideal of the Gospel: "Be perfect, as your heavenly Father is perfect" (Matt. 5:48), and thought that this called for the highest aspirations to transform both individual and collective humanity. His ideas of the organic unity of all knowledge, the integral synthesis of theology, philosophy, and science, and the ultimately spiritual nature of the whole evolutionary process, anticipate many of the insights of the twentieth-century Western mystic Pierre Teilhard de Chardin.

Solovyov's understanding of the whole material world of nature and humanity is one of spiritualization and transfiguration. Like other Orthodox mystics before him, he draws on the

Transfiguration, the awesome, radiant appearance of Christ's body wholly transformed and suffused with light on Mount Tabor (Luke 9:28-36). This event anticipates for him the transfiguration of all material being. Cosmic and historical processes are intimately fused because God, in the person of Christ, has entered the historical process so that divine action in the world is transformative and Christocentric.

Solovyov's deeply mystical experience of faith brings together God's immanence and transcendence with all creation in a grandiose vision of All-Unity where the Absolute contains all within Itself, embracing them all. As he expressed it in an autobiographical poem:

> *Beneath the coarse surface of material being*
> *I managed to touch the eternal purple hue,*
> *And I came to know the radiance of divinity.*

He celebrates God's comprehensive, all-unifying nature, and sees God as Good-Truth-Beauty, believing in the spiritual nature of humanity itself, so that the human being can attain a "plenitude of being." Solovyov's high spiritual ideals were also linked to practical goals, for he worked for reconciliation, defended oppressed groups, especially the Jews, and advocated working for justice and the transformation of society. Rejecting a purely nominal Christianity, he tried to promote an ideal Christian culture, a community of believing Christians, *sobornost,* a community of all within the Church, *one body,* which he equates with Sophia or Divine Wisdom, the true companion of God.

Whereas the Russian intelligentsia of Solovyov's time was largely secularized, and monastic life was greatly curtailed after the Russian Revolution of 1917, a religious renaissance occurred among Russian émigrés to the West in the twentieth century. It led to renewed interest in Orthodox spirituality and mysticism and gave fresh vitality to Orthodox theology. It was in these émigré circles that the idea of *sobornost* was greatly developed. *Sobornost* is an ultimately mystical idea of corporate life and organic unity where each individual, while retaining personal freedom and integrity, can at the same time share in the common life of the whole. Orthodox writers claim *sobornost* as a special characteristic of the Orthodox Church, contrasting it with the greater emphasis on juridical authority in the Roman Catholic Church and the excessive individualism of Protestant Churches. In its fullest sense, *sobornost* is a vision of divine-human wholeness deeply rooted in centuries of Orthodox mystical tradition, a tradition now growing new shoots in our own time.

For millennia, Orthodoxy was not only a faith, but an entire culture. With the collapse of the historical "Orthodox worlds" that were once political empires—Byzantium and Imperial Russia—the Orthodox Church now finds itself in the late twentieth century dispersed in changed societies which represent very different worlds and cultures. The contemporary Orthodox revival of the spiritual vision inherited from Byzantium is not simply a return to the past, but rather a renewal which acts creatively on the present. The new interest in Orthodox spirituality transcends all national, cultural, ethnic, and ecclesiastical boundaries. It is no longer tied to one particular Church or monastic institution, but is growing in all traditionally Orthodox countries as well as in America,

The Optina Pystin monastery, 150 miles southwest of Moscow. This is the hermitage where Tolstoy sought spiritual solace by visiting the *staretzy* (wise monks), and to which Dostoevsky came on pilgrimage after the death of his son.

Western Europe, and other centers of the Orthodox diaspora. The transformative power of this Orthodox spiritual vision, which so much challenges the secularism of our contemporary world, lies more than anything else in the unbroken tradition of Orthodox mystics, whose rich experience and testimony continue to move and inspire right up to the present.

CHAPTER SIX

Mystics of our Time

After the deeply moving unitive experiences, great visions and superb examples of so many Christian mystics of the past, what have the mystics of the twentieth century to give us? How and where do they find union with God in the midst of the modern world? Where is their "desert," their place of centering and stillness, their experience of prayer and contemplation, their life lived "face to face" with God? How have they adapted the traditional practices of asceticism, previous attitudes to the body and the world, and the practice of balancing contemplation with action, to our own time?

Christian mystical experience is by no means a thing of the past. The long tradition of Christian mystics from East and West presented in this book is not merely of historical interest, but has great significance for spiritual life in the contemporary world, a world marked by revolutionary changes and profound transformations affecting ever more human beings around the globe.

Many contemporary mystics exist, both inside and outside the Churches. Modern mystics can be found among Orthodox, Catholic, and Protestant Christians around the world. In fact, there exists a greater number and variety of mystics than ever before, no longer exclusively tied to the monastic and ascetic traditions of the past, although these also continue, but living in very different settings and contexts. The greater variety of mystical figures and paths was already evident among the mystics of the early modern period. The possibility of a mystical vocation for lay people, far removed from monastic and clerical ways of life, is well documented among Protestants, Catholics and Orthodox alike. A good example is found in the previous chapter, in the late-nineteenth-century Orthodox layman Solovyov, who might just as well be counted among the mystics of the modern period.

Modern mystics, with their great variety and individuality, are often "voices at the margin" of traditional Christian institutions. Yet they are inspired by the rich heritage of Christian mysticism handed down by the Churches, and

The Vision after the Sermon, by Paul Gauguin, 1908. Modern painters have often taken religious themes and illustrated them in new ways. In Gauguin's painting, devout Breton women, on leaving the church, have a collective mystical experience and see Jacob wrestling with the angel. (National Gallery of Scotland, Edinburgh)

The thinking of the late-nineteenth-century Russian mystic Solovyov
encompasses many of the concerns and experiences of the present day.

their mystic search, experience, and vision still draw on the great mystical potential of Christian incarnational and sacramental theology. Through the example of their lives and thoughts, these modern mystics inspire others in turn, and thus help to renew and strengthen the sense of a world-wide Christian community whose greatest ideal still remains to seek and love God above all, and to witness to the ever-present divine Spirit among us by helping to create a world of greater wholeness, peace, and justice, with profound reverence for all of creation.

The early Christian and medieval mystics are much easier to discuss than modern ones, because so often only the most essential and valuable parts of their experience have been preserved as pearls of wisdom handed down to future generations. The nearer we move to our own time, the more difficult it becomes to separate the jewels of mystical splendor from all the dross of daily life, from all the myriad details that an age of communications can now preserve through print and image. We not only possess many more spiritual and mystic figures, but we also know so much more about the mystics of the late nineteenth and twentieth centuries.

Thus it is particularly difficult, if not impossible, to make a representative choice, for there are so many mystical writers we can encounter in the modern period, people who are widely known, venerated, and loved, whose examples, heroic and humble, are an inspiration to thousands of others. I will briefly mention several different modern mystics, chosen for the variety of approaches and insights they represent, and then concentrate on three unusual figures of the twentieth century.

One of the best-known and most loved modern mystics of Roman Catholicism is **St. Thérèse of Lisieux** (1873-97), also known as the Little Flower or St. Theresa of the Child Jesus. She was born into a deeply religious family, and her intense piety developed early. She entered the Carmelite convent in Lisieux at an unusually young age, and suffered from nervous disabilities all her life. But in wrestling with her scruples, doubts and struggles she became a saint who described her method of loving and finding God as "the way of spiritual childhood, the way of trust and surrender." After an early death from tuberculosis her mystical autobiography *The Story of a Soul* was published and has become a modern spiritual classic.

Humble, insignificant, "little," as she perceived herself, Thérèse was in some ways a rather traditional woman, marked by that female obedience and dutiful submissiveness which were part of nineteenth-century bourgeois expectations. Yet there was another tenacious and irrepressible side to her character, evident from her strong will and wishes, impossible to realize, to be a missionary perhaps, or above all a priest. Her "little way" of prayer has become a message for our time, so that after her all too brief life Thérèse has grown into one of the most popular saints, from whom many people draw strength and encouragement.

Another influential figure from around the turn of the century is Brother **Charles de Foucauld** (1858-1916). In contrast to Thérèse's bourgeois background, he came from the French aristocracy. Although brought up in a devout family, as a young man he lost his faith and squandered his fortune in living as a dandy *de la belle epoque*. He eventually trained as a soldier, but after a conversion experience in 1886, he

became a Trappist monk and contemplative. Jesus became the passion of his life, so much so that he chose to be a hermit in the North African desert, in Algeria, where he tried to live in the spirit of life in Nazareth.

He endeared himself to the Tuareg tribes, compiled the first Tuareg grammar and dictionary, translated the Gospels and transcribed Tuareg proverbs and love songs. In a tragic misunderstanding he was killed during the First World War by anti-French tribesmen. Yet his solitary life and mystical spirituality have exercised a lasting influence on our time. Brother Charles was a man of deep contemplative prayer, focused above all on the eucharistic presence of Jesus. He wrote thousands of meditations alive with freshness and simplicity, and the fervor of his example inspired the foundation of the Little Sisters and Little Brothers of Jesus.

A completely different example is the British Jesuit **Gerard Manley Hopkins** (1844-89), who became known only many years after his death for his spiritual poetry, with its mystical vision of the world "filled with the grandeur of God."

Charles de Foucauld's spiritual experience in the desert forges a link with that of the earliest Christian mystics. Paradoxically, his example inspired the creation of new religious communities in contemporary urban settings.

St. Thérèse of Lisieux, by Edouard Maxence, 1928. Thérèse, a Carmelite nun, died at the age of twenty-four. The intense mystical piety and "little way of prayer" of this modern saint have attracted many contemporary followers. (Private Collection)

Raised as an Anglican, he converted to Roman Catholicism as a student after coming under the influence of the Oxford Movement, and was received into the Church by John Henry Newman. He had such a distinguished academic record that Benjamin Jowett described him as the "star of Balliol" at Oxford, but Hopkins chose to enter the Jesuits in 1868 and was ordained in 1877.

After first working in various parishes and a Jesuit school, he became a lecturer at University College in Dublin. He found Ireland uncongenial, and experienced a great sense of desolation and spiritual aridity, which found expression in his poems. At that time only his friends knew of his writing, and praised him, after his death from typhoid fever in 1889, for his great personal integrity and rare "chastity of mind." Hopkins's poems express the intensity of his religious feelings, his reflections on his vocation as a Jesuit priest, his deep sense of God's mystery, grandeur, and mercy, his joy in "all things counter, original, intense, spare, strange." Hopkins responded vividly to the beauty of nature and, with great subtlety of perception, created poems in a highly original style, thus giving powerful expression to a deeply mystical vision of the world.

Yet another British figure is the mystical poet,

Gerard Manley Hopkins, the late nineteenth-century English poet and mystic who speaks directly to our age.

Evelyn Underhill was a modern "mistress of the spiritual life." She exercized much influence through leading retreats, and her seminal studies on the mystics are still widely read.

author and scholar **Evelyn Underhill** (1875-1941). She was so deeply involved with mystical experience that she wrote one of the first major studies on it, the magisterial *Mysticism* (1911), which has exercized a lasting influence on contemporary discussions of the subject. Together with her works on *The Mystic Way* (1913) and *Worship* (1936), this book helped to establish mystical theology as a respectable discipline among the intellectuals of her time.

A lifelong Anglican, Evelyn Underhill was always strongly attracted to Roman Catholic piety and religious experience. The Roman Catholic writer Baron von Hügel, also an authority on Christian mysticism, acted as her spiritual director for many years. By the 1940s, Underhill had come to focus more on the sacramental elements in Christianity, and her theology then became entirely centered on a powerful experience of Christ. She gained a reputation as a leading religious counselor and retreat leader; she was also a frequent lecturer at conferences and seminars, wrote two books on poetry and did journalistic work. Of a deeply mystical temperament herself, she is above all remembered for her pioneering work in the scholarship of mysticism and for her classification of mystical experience, based on mystics drawn from the Jewish, Christian, Muslim, and Indian traditions. Personally so much concerned with spiritual practice and direction, the nature of worship and the importance of retreats, she has strongly influenced the contemporary retreat movement.

Less well known perhaps is the German Carmelite nun **Edith Stein** (1891-1942), a Roman Catholic convert from Judaism. Born into a wealthy Jewish family, she became an atheist when still very young, studied philosophy, and was so gifted that the philosopher Edmund Husserl invited her to become his assistant in his work on phenomenology. She obtained a doctorate in philosophy and was later introduced to Roman Catholicism. It was particularly her profound encounter with Teresa of Avila's autobiography at a friend's house that led to her conversion in 1921. She gave up her university post and worked in various schools and later at the University of Münster, which she had to leave in 1932 because of her Jewish background.

In 1934 she joined a Carmelite convent and took the name of Sister Teresa Benedicta of the Cross. She continued with her philosophical writing and produced a phenomenological study of St. John of the Cross. In 1942 she was seized by the Gestapo and taken, with her sister Rosa, to the concentration camp of Auschwitz, where both women were killed.

Steeped in the thought of John of the Cross, Edith Stein's spirituality was deeply mystical. Her major study *The Science of the Cross* captures the power of St. John's love mysticism and theology of the cross in a Europe devastated by

The late Dag Hammarskjöld was a fine example of contemplation in action and of mystical consciousness in the midst of a busy modern world.

the horrors of war, destruction and organized mass genocide. Survivors of the Auschwitz atrocities who met Edith during her brief period in the camp have testified to her courage and the great compassion with which she helped other sufferers.

A very different figure, one of great action but imbued with deep mystical consciousness, is **Dag Hammarskjöld** (1905-61), the Swedish economist and statesman who was the second Secretary General of the United Nations. Under his leadership the UN gained greatly in prestige and effectiveness, for Hammarskjöld was a highly practical peacemaker. He met a tragic death while on a peace mission to the Congo, when the plane on which he was traveling crashed over what is now Zambia. Posthumously, in 1961, he was awarded the Nobel Peace Price.

Hammarskjöld was known as a remote and deeply private man, but he left a spiritual diary, *Markings,* published after his death. He has described these notes as "a sort of *white book* concerning my negotiations with myself—and with God." They reflect his inner experiences and religious thoughts between

1925 and 1961, but also include passages from the Bible and the mystics, such as "Faith is the marriage of God and the Soul (St. John of the Cross)." He describes in his own words walking "with God through the deep places of creation" in a dream, or again, "Thou takest the pen—and the lines dance. Thou takest the flute—and the notes shimmer. Thou takest the brush—and the colors sing. So all things have meaning and beauty in that space beyond time where Thou art. How, then, can I hold back anything from Thee?"

If Hammarskjöld's mystic way was expressed through service to others, the importance of the social dimension in a deeply mystical faith is even more explicitly articulated in the spiritual reflections of the black American theologian **Howard Thurman** (1899-1981), described as "a modern mystic and prophet." A Christian minister and theology professor at Howard University, in Washington D.C., he produced many publications. In one of them he has described his grandmother's experience as a slave whose identity and dignity

DEEP RIVER

Reflections on the Religious Insight of Certain of the Negro Spirituals

HOWARD THURMAN

Illustrated by Elizabeth Orton Jones

HARPER & BROTHERS·
New York

Title page of *Deep River*, by Howard Thurman. Thurman's deeply mystical faith and his inspiring writings are a great source of empowerment for African-American Christians.

were upheld by the belief that all people are children of God. His own experience is recounted in his spiritual autobiography *With Head and Heart* (1979). Among his other works must be mentioned *Meditations of the Heart* (1953) and *The Inward Journey* (1961), whereas his inspiring reflections on the relationship between religion and racism are found in his earlier *Jesus and the Disinherited* (1949).

For Thurman, the religion of Jesus provides hope for the disinherited, the dispossessed, and the poor of society, because it is centered on a love-ethic which makes true fellowship possible. This love-ethic is the way to God and overcomes the contradictions of life. A person's true worth is not determined by race or nationality, but by the divine status of being a child of God. Jesus was born a poor Jew, and his religion can offer love to poor, desperate people. The religion of Jesus inspires courage in the midst of despair; it gives hope to develop resistance, and provides inner strength which can truly transform, so that inward integrity can be shared by all. When the depth of the soul is touched, a universal spirit is found that includes all people.

The best-known modern mystic is probably the American monk **Thomas Merton** (1915-68). A powerful witness to the continuing vitality of Christian spirituality in the modern world, he has been called the most influential proponent of traditional monasticism in American history. His mother was American and his father a New Zealander. Born in the French *Midi,* he received his education in France, followed by university in England, at Cambridge. While living there he led a somewhat dissolute life; he drank, had several girlfriends, and eventually fathered a child (it is rumored that mother and child were killed during the blitz). He continued his studies at Columbia University, New York, and, after reading Gilson's *The Spirit of Medieval Philosophy,* converted to Catholicism. He applied for admission to the Franciscan Order but was rejected. Eventually he joined the Abbey of Our Lady of Gethsemani in Kentucky, a monastery of the Cistercians of the Strict Observance, better known as Trappists. Soon afterwards he published his spiritual autobiography, *The Seven Storey Mountain* (an image taken from Dante), which became a huge success and brought him into international prominence. He wrote about contemplative prayer in *Seeds of Contemplation,* followed by many other works such as *Waters of Siloe, The Ascent to Truth* and *New Seeds of Contemplation.*

Merton is one of the most influential contemporary spiritual writers. Few in our time have spoken so inspiringly of the "deep movements of love" that come in the highest reaches of contemplation. His writings reveal a deep familiarity with the tradition of Catholic mystical theology, but he also came under the influence of Eastern mysticism, particularly that of Zen Buddhism. In 1968 he traveled to the East, met the Dalai Lama, and participated in a monastic renewal conference in Bangkok where he accidentally died. His powerful impressions of Asia, containing deep spiritual insights, are recorded in his posthumously published *Asian Journal.*

For him, the task of contemplation is one of self-emptying so that God can take full possession of the human being. The first step to contemplation is faith, which begins with an ascent to Christ's teaching through his Church. Contemplation is the union of the human mind and will with God in an act of pure love which brings us into obscure contact with God as he really is:

> *In meditation we do not seek to know about God as though he were an object like other objects which submit to our scrutiny and can be expressed in clear scientific ideas. We seek to know God himself, beyond the level of all the objects which he has made...The infinite God has no boundaries and our minds cannot set limits to him or to his love.*

For Merton, Christian contemplation supersedes every other form of contemplation, whether in art, philosophy, theology, or liturgy. Action and contemplation are not opposed to each other but are two aspects of the same love of God.

Merton was like a hermit "living with wisdom" in the modern world. He left an extraordinary spiritual legacy from which continue to come forth poems, letters and

Thomas Merton and the Dalai Lama in 1968. Merton is one the most influential contemporary spiritual writers. His conception of Christian contemplation combined Catholic mystical theology with the profound insights of Zen Buddism.

articles to this day, and a number of groups have come into existence which are devoted to the study of his thought and spiritual practice.

Besides the modern mystics discussed briefly so far, it is worth considering three more figures in greater detail. They represent both continuity and contrast to the previous ones, while also being very different from each other. But they also stand out as different from the earlier mystics in the Christian tradition because each of them introduces a new element into mystical spirituality and practice. These three mystics are Simone Weil, Teilhard de Chardin, and Swami Abhishiktananda.

Simone Weil (1909-43)

It might seem incongruous at first to include a French Jewish writer in a book on Christian mystics, but Simone Weil is a splendid example of the pluriform expression that mystical experience finds in the modern world. Radical in her political and social thought, she was deeply drawn to the Catholic Church, so much so that some consider her a true Christian at heart, even though she never formally converted. She upheld such uncompromisingly high standards for being a Christian that she not only felt unworthy, but also found it impossible to join a Church full of blemishes. Her essays on spirituality deal with the love of God and the spiritual demands of such love. Nowhere is this more movingly expressed than in her book *Waiting for God,* a modern spiritual classic which is subtitled "The essence of her thought." Other famous works are *The Need for Roots, Gravity and Grace,* and her *First and Last Notebooks.*

Born into an agnostic Jewish family in Paris,

Simone Weil studied at the *École Normale Supérieure* and became a philosophy teacher who soon turned into a political activist. She took a job at the Renault car factory in order to learn through her own experience about the hard conditions of the workers, and subsequently spent some time at the Catalonian front sharing the sufferings of the Republican army during the Spanish Civil War. She wrote for political journals of the left and periodically took on manual labor out of solidarity with the poor and exploited in society.

Three experiences of Catholic life moved her deeply: the celebration of a saint's festival in a Portuguese village, an occasion of prayer in Assisi, and above all the Easter week liturgy at the Benedictine Abbey of Solesmes, with the unimaginable beauty of the chanting of its monks. She had a profound mystical experience then in which she felt that the Passion of Christ entered her whole being. This made her realize "the possibility of loving divine love in the midst of affliction," both themes on which she subsequently reflected and wrote a great deal.

During her stay at Solesmes, an Englishman conveyed to her something about the transformative power of the eucharist and drew her attention to the metaphysical poets. When she read them, she became particularly attracted to George Herbert's mystical poem *Love,* which she learned by heart, reciting it regularly with all her attention focused on it while fighting her violent headaches, from which she suffered so much. It was during one of these recitations that she underwent one of her most powerful inner experiences. "Christ came down and took me," she later simply wrote, describing him as having taken possession of her in the deepest center of

Simone Weil, here seen in uniform during the Spanish Civil War. Of Jewish origin, she became deeply attracted to Christianity, though she never joined the Church. She found the love of God in the midst of much suffering, and was devoted to the figure of Christ.

her soul, without her senses or imagination having any part. According to her own account she had never read the work of any mystics until then, nor could she have foreseen the possibility of a real contact "person to person, here below, between a human being and God." It seemed that God invaded her being and broke down her barriers and defences. All her attention and waiting had found an answer.

Subsequently she also learned the Christian prayer "Our Father" by heart, and recited it equally attentively in its original Greek form. Again, she writes, the words tore her thoughts from her body so that she found herself transported to "a place outside space where there is neither perspective nor point of view." She felt filled with infinity and the fullness of silence beyond the absence of sound. On other occasions she experienced the total presence of Christ "infinitely more real, more moving, more clear than on that first occasion when he took possession of me."

Simone Weil's intense devotion to the suffering Christ became central to her writings on "affliction." She shows in her work how all aspects of experience can be creatively transformed into channels of waiting for divine presence and grace. All human activities and experiences, whatever they are, can become a way and means for loving God, but God's own disclosure is ultimately utterly gratuitous. For her, "The beauty of the world is Christ's tender smile for us coming through matter." Like Teresa of Ávila, Simone Weil uses the image of the soul as a garden and God as the gardener who puts a seed in the ground of our soul. We have to wait upon this seed whose growth, however, is often accompanied by pain.

The ancient Abbey of Solesmes on the River Sarthe, southwest of Le Mans. It was here that Simone Weil discovered and learned George Herbert's mystical poem *Love*. Recitation of this poem later led to one of her deepest mystical experiences.

In 1942 Weil left France with her family to escape anti-Semitic policies. She first went to the United States, but then traveled to England to work with the French government in exile. When she became ill, she refused to take the food she needed out of solidarity with the French people suffering under German occupation. Her health fast deteriorated, and she died soon afterwards in Ashford, in Kent, at the young age of thirty-four.

Simone Weil was much influenced by her study of classical Greek philosophy, but also developed such an intense interest in Indian philosophy and religion that she learnt Sanskrit in order to read the *Bhagavad Gita* in the original. She wrote with power about the unprecedented times in which we live, in a world crying out for God, with people in spiritual peril in every part of the globe. She calls with great urgency for a truly incarnate Christianity and the development of a new kind of saintliness. Like some other modern mystics, Simone Weil believed that the rootless, spirit-bereft character of the contemporary world demands a new kind of mystic-prophetic spirituality-in-the-world struggling for justice and peace.

This perspective would have found much support from her compatriot Pierre Teilhard de Chardin, had he known her. He too writes most movingly about the empowering presence of God in all things but, unlike her, he develops his mystical insights not on the basis of philosophy, but on that of modern science.

Pierre Teilhard de Chardin (1881-1955)

Born in the Auvergne into an aristocratic French family distantly related to Voltaire, the young Pierre was much influenced by the deep religious faith of his mother, who first introduced him to the Christian mystics. His father, interested in natural history, encouraged him from a young age to collect stones, rocks and bones, which laid the foundations for his later career as a geologist and paleontologist. All through his life Teilhard's two vocations—the ardent love of God and his vibrant passion for the natural and human world—were held in tension and balance, producing an essentially "new type

of mysticism, the result of a profound, life-long, reconciling meditation on religion and scientific truth." For him, science itself became tinged with mysticism and charged with faith.

One of eleven children, Teilhard grew up in a closely knit family which shared intimate warmth and joy, but also much suffering, pain, and loss. As a young child he already experienced a deep sense of oneness, later followed by mystical natural experiences linked to the "vast open spaces" of sea and desert, but also the riches of fossil life which made him ecstatically perceive "that through all of nature I was immersed in God." For him Jesus "comes to us clothed in the glory of the world."

Educated by Jesuits, Teilhard joined the Jesuit Order as a young man. He spent his early years studying in Jesuit houses in Jersey and Hastings, where he was ordained in 1911. He had previously spent several years teaching in a Jesuit college in Egypt, and after completing the study of theology he took up advanced scientific research in Paris. This was interrupted by serving as a stretcher-bearer in the trenches of the First World War, largely with a North African regiment. Almost daily at the boundary of life and death, he saw the war as a crucible of fire which forged all his experiences together into one powerful vision of God and the world which, from then onwards, he described in numerous writings, often with great lyrical beauty.

An equally formative experience was his encounter with the immense continent and "fermenting mass of the peoples of Asia," where he first went on a scientific expedition in 1923. The vastness of Mongolia led him "to the heart of the unique greatness of God," and it was there that he wrote his famous *Mass on the World*, a

Pierre Teilhard de Chardin, a great explorer, scientist, and mystic, found the heart of
God at the heart of the physical world.

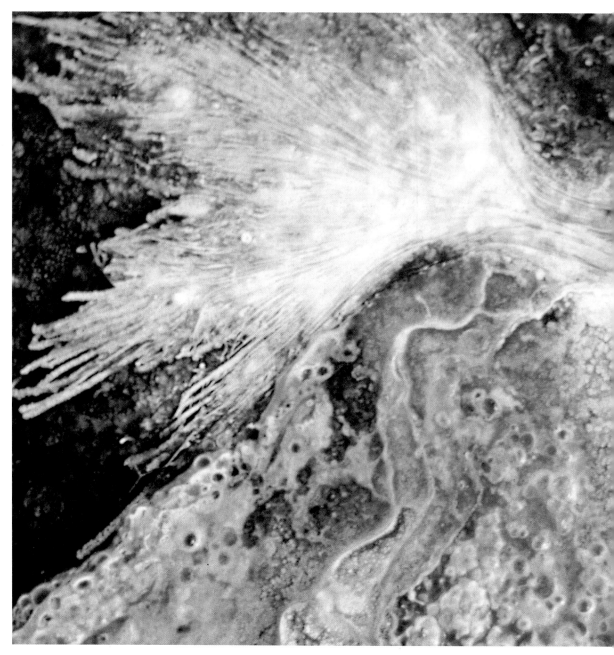

Patterns in nature—sulphur ore. Teilhard de Chardin's mystical vision takes us up into the ever-moving stream of life inherent in all matter. He experienced this universal becoming as an all-pervasive energy which vividly conveyed to him the intimate presence of God, and the incandescent fire of the Spirit.

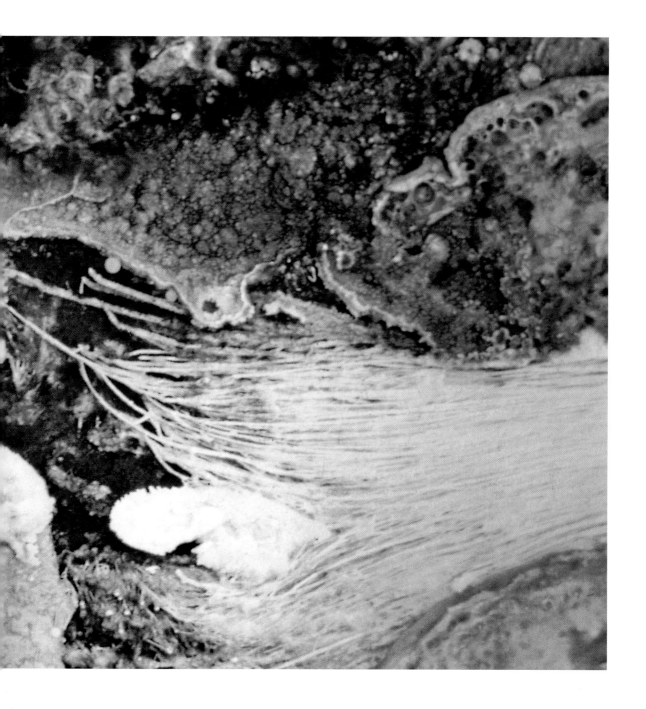

deeply mystical and sacramental offering of the travails of the world transformed and transfigured by the fire of the divine Spirit.

Deeply influenced by evolution, Teilhard saw all becoming as centered in the "cosmic Christ" and experienced the presence of God in all things as a "divine milieu" which surrounds us everywhere. His lyrical mysticism and great vision of humanity coming together in one "noosphere"—a layer of mind, action, and love connecting all human beings and encircling the globe—was conceived in the cataclysmic experiences of the trenches, and then further developed through his scientific

Teilhard de Chardin visiting the Ming tombs outside Peking, accompanied by the great prehistorian Abbé Breuil. The great open spaces of Asia were a formative influence on Teilhard's cosmic mysticism.

work, his travels and his contact with Eastern religions. His deeply Christocentric, incarnational mysticism, understood as an intimate, Christic element present in matter and its becoming, was expressed with fervor and devotion, from his first writing in 1916 to his last in 1955. "The presence of the Incarnate Word penetrates everything, as a universal element, it shines at the common heart of things, as a center that is infinitely intimate to them and at the same time...infinitely distant."

Teilhard had a brilliant scientific career,

pursued for over twenty years in China, in Europe, and in America, including several visits to India, Indonesia, Burma, Japan, North and Southern Africa, and to South America. But his religious ideas were found to be unorthodox and dangerous by the Catholic Church, and he was not allowed to publish anything during his lifetime except his scientific works. When his best-known, but perhaps also one of his most difficult books, *The Phenomenon of Man*, was first published after his death in 1955, it immediately became a best-seller; but he has exercized a more powerful impact on many people inside and outside the Churches today through his writings on spirituality and mysticism. Even the Vatican has expressed some approval of Teilhard's ideas in retrospect. In comparison to other spiritual writers of today, however, his powerful vision of a passionate involvement with the dynamic realities of our physical and social world, and of the "spirit of one earth" where the age of nations is passed, is far too little known. Many of his views provide strong connections to contemporary discussions about religion and science, ecology and interfaith dialog, and even bear on aspects of feminism and globalization. He was a daring pioneer of great originality and insight in many fields, although there is also much in his thought that remains undeveloped and open to criticism.

Teilhard combines science and mysticism in teaching a mysticism of action and transformation by "communion with God through the world." In his life and work, action and contemplation are integrated in a dynamic balance linked to the "divinization" of our activities and passivities, as is evident from his essay on the interior life, *The Divine Milieu.* His spiritual autobiography, *The Heart of Matter,* is an inspiring testimony to the fire of the Spirit; also moving is the *Hymn of the Universe,* a collection of some of his earliest and most poetic writings.

Teilhard writes stirringly about God's universal presence, which he calls "the divine diaphany" in all things. Throughout all the vicissitudes of his life he remained single-mindedly focused on the one and "only thing needful" to give meaning and direction, unswerving hope, trust, and love: the empowering spark of divine presence which was alive in him until the end. "Throughout my life, by means of my life, the world has little by little caught fire in my sight until, aflame all around me, it has become almost luminous from within… Such has been my experience in contact with the earth—the diaphany of the Divine at the heart of a universe on fire."

During the later years of his life, Teilhard de Chardin's thoughts were much occupied with the urgent need to develop the spiritual energy resources needed by the human community for sustaining human life and assuring its future.

From his deeply religious and mystical perspective, this could be achieved only through the powers of love. Love alone can create stronger, more permanent bonds between all human beings, and between humanity and God. Thus he wrote: "Some day after mastering the wind, the waves, and gravity, we shall harness for God the energies of Love, and then for the second time in history we will have discovered Fire."

Teilhard de Chardin was truly a modern mystic of fire, of divine energy, light, and life. He realized early that the spiritual energy resources available to us today, however much rooted in distinct religious streams, have to be drawn from all the different world faiths. When he first went to the Far East, he was hoping for a renewal of Christianity, especially through contact with Buddhism, and greatly admired the vision of Oneness found in Indian religions. But he himself never developed these ideas very much. It was others who, existentially and mystically, immersed themselves in the depth experience of another faith. One such figure was Henri le Saux, better known as Swami Abhishiktananda.

Swami Abhishiktananda (Henri le Saux) (1910-73)

Henri le Saux was a pioneer in Hindu-Christian dialog who explored spiritual frontiers to which few had ventured until then. Early attracted to Indian spirituality, this French Benedictine spent nearly twenty years in a monastery in France before going to India in 1948, where he joined **Abbé Jules Monchanin** (1895-1957). The latter had been in India since the late thirties, working in a South Indian Christian diocese for several years. He wanted to become as Indian as possible in an attempt to purify his faith and recapture the original spirit of Christianity. In particular, he planned to establish a Christian ashram, a place of retreat on the Hindu model, entirely devoted to contemplation and representing a Christian integration of the Hindu monastic tradition.

When Henri le Saux arrived in India, Monchanin was able to go ahead with his plan. The two men were given some land on the banks of the sacred Kavery river in Tamil Nadu, where they founded the first Catholic ashram in India which they dedicated to the Trinity. They called it *Saccidananda Ashram,* using the Hindu term for the Absolute, conceived as *Sat* (Being), *Cit* (Consciousness), and *Ananda* (Bliss). This name expressed their intention of identifying the Hindu quest of the Absolute with their own experience of God in Christ in the mystery of the Holy Trinity. The Ashram, usually better known as *Shantivanam* (Forest of Peace), initially followed a Benedictine pattern of life, but became increasingly Indian in style. The two priests adopted the dress of *sannyasins*—wandering Hindu holy men who have renounced the world—and took Indian names. Dom le Saux became known as Swami Abhishiktananda (Bliss of the Anointed One),

The French Benedictine Dom le Saux immersed himself in Indian spirituality during his many years in India. He took the Hindu name Swami Abhishiktananda, and integrated in his experience the best of Christian and Indian mysticism.

Swami being the title of an Indian holy man.

Swami Abhishiktananda, like the desert fathers before him, felt a strong call to renunciation, and was much influenced by two Indian sages, Sri Ramana Maharishi and Sri Gnanananda, whom he visited between 1949 and 1957. He left Shantivanam in 1968 to become a hermit in the Himalayas, living there until his death in 1973 and attracting one disciple, who also lived as a hermit.

Swami Abhishiktananda followed the path of a *sannyasin,* drawn to the Advaitic experience of the highest Self, the One-without-a-second. His special calling was to live his own dedication to Christ from within the depth of this Hindu spirituality, a calling lived out in "the cave of the heart," as he used to say.

Swami Abhishiktananda never left India again, and later took Indian nationality. He stayed in many Hindu ashrams, went on several pilgrimages across India, and especially in the Himalayas, got involved with Christian ecumenical retreats and prayer meetings, and was deeply committed to combining the Christian Trinitarian experience of God with the Hindu Vedanta realization of the Absolute. He became a Christian Guru who exercized a considerable influence on many Westerners

Contemporary bronze statue of the Hindu god Shiva as Nataraja, Lord of the Dance, who destroys the world at the end of time. In a different personification Shiva maintains the world by his meditations. Beneath its diversity and complexity, the underlying unity of Hinduism has correspondences with the inward dimension of the Christian faith. (Oriental Museum, Durham University, England)

interested in Hindu-Christian encounter at the deepest mystical level. His work at Shantivanam was later carried on by the British Benedictine **Father Bede Griffith** (1906-93), who has perhaps had an even greater influence on Western people seeking a mystical spirituality that is truly alive to the contemporary world.

Abhishiktananda distinguished between the different Advaita philosophies and an underlying Advaitic experience. While he remained keenly aware of the deep tension between the two different spiritualities of Christianity and Vedanta, he immersed himself in the Indian experience and was willing to give up the support of all names and forms, including the name and form of the Lord. He sought to penetrate the mystical experience of East and West at the deepest level and believed that Christianity would be renewed from its contact with Hindu spirituality. He spiritualized his Himalayan pilgrimage in being drawn to "the summit which instinctively connects with the dwelling place of God." By "seeking the source" of the Ganges high up in the mountains, he was getting in touch also with those spiritual waters which issue from high peaks and can feed and sustain human life.

Swami Abhishiktananda's experience included the belief that there is an Advaitic dimension, an experience of deep, underlying unity, in Christianity itself which must be recovered. Some of his experience of Hindu-Christian dialog and deep mystical reflection are captured in his writings on *Prayer, Hindu-Christian Meeting Point, Saccidananda: A Christian Approach to Advaitic Experience* and in his posthumously published diaries. He was convinced that the Advaitic experience calls into question not the heart of the Christian faith, but only too external an understanding of it. At the center there is a deeper level of meeting in the Spirit to which we can all relate. As he wrote in his book *The Further Shore*:

> *The Spirit blows where he will. He calls from within, he calls from without. May his chosen ones never fail to attend to his call! In the desert or in the jungle, just as much as in the world, the danger is always to fix one's attention upon oneself. For the wise man, who has discovered his true Self, there is no longer either forest or town, clothes or nakedness, doing or not-doing. He has the freedom of the Spirit, and through him the Spirit works as he wills in this world, using equally his silence and his speech, his solitude and his presence in society. Having passed beyond his "own" self, his "own" life, his "own" being and doing, he finds bliss and peace in the Self alone, the only real Self.*

For Swami Abhishiktananda the Christian mystic's "experience of the Self leads on to the Trinitarian experience of *Saccidananda*," fully knowing that this conviction depends on faith alone. He considered it an important further step in the development of Christianity that "it will accept what is essential in the Advaitic experience and penetrate to its very heart; and yet it will still remain itself, or even find itself anew precisely in those ultimate depths of the Spirit to which Advaita calls it."

From a long tradition of Christian monasticism, Henri le Saux found his way to God through radical renunciation and surrender, by stripping away all externals and meeting Hinduism on the path of *jnana,* or wisdom,

Indian Christians worshiping in Goa. Western missionaries first brought traditional Christianity to India, but Indian Christians are now exploring new spiritual directions through closer contact with Hinduism, a development of great importance for Christianity all over the world.

taught by the ancient *Upanishads*, the last section of the *Vedas*, the sacred literature of Brahmanical Hinduism. He realized a profoundly personal synthesis of Hindu-Christian spirituality in his own life. Others are following the same path of meditation, that of *bhakti,* or devotion, advocated by the *Bhagavad Gita,* the "Song of the Lord," the best-known and most popular of Hindu religious writings. Yet others experience deep points of Christian renewal through an in-depth dialog with Buddhism, Islam, Judaism, or the great primal religions of the world. The future of Christian mysticism is wide open. Sources of renewal can be found in all the wisdom traditions of the world. For Christians a creative return to the center of their own tradition will always mean to discover afresh the splendor of God's love in Christ, the presence of the Spirit among us, and the mystery of the Trinity which is one of deepest union and communion—the ultimate summit of all Christian mystic life.

CONCLUSION

Christian mysticism is still alive. Though little known outside the Christian world, the fire of the mystics still burns, and their ardent vision continues to attract other seekers searching for the same light. The richness of these mystics is as inexhaustible as God's life and Spirit itself. Their example can give us peace, joy, and zest for life, with a depth of meaning that we desperately need. Yet we must ask, if we are honest, what meaning this rich tradition of Christian mystics can have for women and men living fully in the world of today. And in what form will this mystical heritage be handed down to future generations, living in the next century and beyond?

Western Christians have rediscovered the contemplative traditions of Eastern Orthodoxy, and many people in the West, whether religious or not, are being greatly enriched by the wisdom of the mystical traditions of the East. In the past, Christian mystical experience was closely linked to asceticism and monasticism, to a great tradition of learning about earlier mystics, and to

following the instructions of a spiritual guide or master. In our century, the Taizé community of the Reformed Protestant tradition, founded in the 1940s in France, is an example of modern monastic renewal. In contemporary Western monasticism there exists a trend towards a much greater individualism, which reinterprets the fundamental Christian tradition in the light of personal experience. Both Thomas Merton and Swami Abhishiktananda are good examples of this. The question arises, however, whether the future of Christian mysticism will primarily be linked to a monastic renewal and an interfaith encounter among monks and nuns, as some seem to think, or whether mystical experience will occur in a much more diffuse, individualistic way, as was the case with some of the modern mystics of the Protestant tradition, and with Evelyn Underhill, Simone Weil, Dag Hammarskjöld, Howard Thurman, and other mystics of the twentieth century.

There is no doubt that the deepest renewal of Christianity can come only from a deeply spiritual and mystic renewal. As Swami

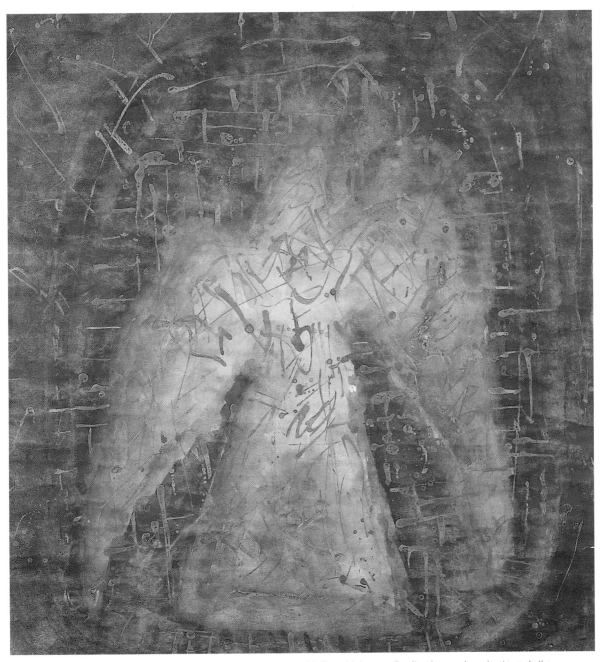

Golden Bird Rising, by Peter Davidson, 1992. The human soul is like a bird, spreading its wings and soaring towards the brilliant light of divine splendor and God's all-enfolding love. (Private Collection)

Abhishiktananda wrote in his *Hindu-Christian Meeting Point*: "As more and more Christians become deeply familiar with the mystics and their writings, the contemplative dimension of the faith, which, though latent, is present at the heart of the Church, will gradually be brought to light. Then her rites, institutions and formularies, the life of her members—in a word, her whole 'epiphany,' the entire 'revelation' of the Lord which by her very calling she exists to show forth in the world—will be increasingly permeated with the spirit of contemplation and interiority.

Only at this depth of interiority will it be possible for the Church to solve realistically and effectively the problems with which she is faced today."

The history of Christian mystics is extraordinarily rich, with numerous colorful personalities from many contrasting back-grounds. Lay and cleric, ascetics and monastics, married men and women in all walks of life, the great company of Christian mystics all attest to the fact that union with God can be searched for and found, whoever and wherever we are. Yet not all mystics speak to us in the same convincing way. Their life of asceticism and renunciation, with its rejection of so much that is human, its denial of world and body, is often excessively dualistic, and in it we do not always see the integral wholeness we seek.

Thus there is a need for a new mysticism in a new world. Creative mystics are necessary to adapt the heritage of the past to the needs of a new season. In the past, the wisdom and insight of mystical knowledge have been handed down within the Christian Church and tied to its doctrines. But today the situation is much more experimental and open-ended. We live in a largely secular and religiously plural world, where the treasures of all religions are being opened like a nut, so that their precious kernels can be discovered and shared by all. Traditional wisdom speaks to us not only across the ages, but also across different religions, so that during our new experience of interfaith encounter, the unending mystical vision quest of men and women from different faiths can enlighten and inspire us in a more enriching and complex way than ever before.

"The force that through the green fuse drives the flower..."
The water lilley, rooted in the mud, grows towards the light, a metaphor for spiritual transcendence.

BIBLIOGRAPHY

For easily accessible selections and complete editions of works by Christian mystics, see:

Bowie, Fiona, ed. *Beguine Spirituality. An Anthology.* London: SPCK, 1989.

Davies, Oliver, ed. *The Rhineland Mystics. An Anthology.* London: SPCK, 1989.

Fleming, David A., ed. *The Fire and the Cloud. An Anthology of Catholic Spirituality. Basic writings by the great mystics of history.* The Missionary Society of St. Paul the Apostle in the State of New York and London: Chapman, 1978.

Grant, Patrick. *A Dazzling Darkness. An Anthology of Western Mysticism.* London: Collins Fount Paperbacks, 1985.

King, Ursula. *Spirit of Fire. The Life and Vision of Teilhard de Chardin.* Maryknoll, New York: Orbis Books, 1996.

Magill, Frank N. & Ian P. McGreal, eds. *Christian Spirituality. The Essential Guide to the Most Influential Spiritual Writings of the Christian Tradition.* San Francisco: Harper & Row, 1988.

The Classics of Western Spirituality. An important series of the works of individual Christian mystics. New York: Paulist Press, and London: SPCK (continuing series).

For a historical overview and a greater in-depth study of the Christian mystical tradition, see:

Cox, Michael. *A Handbook of Christian Mysticism.* London: The Aquarian Press, 1986.

Happold, F. C. *Mysticism. A Study and an Anthology.* Harmondsworth, England: Penguin Books, 1971.

Jones, Cheslyn, Geoffrey Wainwright & Edward Yarnold, eds. *The Study of Spirituality.* London: SPCK, 1986.

zum Brunn, Emilie, & Georgette Epiney-Burgard. *Women Mystics in Medieval Europe.* New York: Paragon House, 1989.

For an encyclopedic history of the religious quest, see:

McGinn, Bernard, & John Meyendorff, eds. *Christian Spirituality I: Origins to the Twelfth Century.* London: Routledge & Kegan Paul, 1986.

Raitt, Jill, ed. *Christian Spirituality II: High Middle Ages and Reformation.* London: Routledge & Kegan Paul, 1987.

Dupré, Louis, & Don E. Saliers, eds. *Christian Spirituality III: Post-Reformation and Modern.* London: SCM Press, 1989.

The interior of the Bell Harry tower in Canterbury Cathedral, England, late fifteenth century.

INDEX

Out of the Deep, enamel pendant by the Scottish artist Phoebe Anna Traquair, 1908. All mystics believe in the power of the Divine, here represented as an angel, drawing us out of the depths into the fullness of the light and life of the Spirit. (The Royal Museum of Scotland, Edinburgh)

ACKNOWLEDGMENTS

In the writing of this book, the author has drawn on the work of many scholars. Brief quotations have been taken from the following, full details of which are given in the Bibliography:

Cox, Michael, *A Handbook of Christian Mysticism*, quoted on pp.57, 108, 109, 116, 128, 163.

Davies, Oliver, ed., *The Rhineland Mystics*, quoted on pp. 104, 106 (twice).

Dupré, Louis, & Don E. Saliers, eds., *Christian Spirituality III*, quoted on pp. 151, 152.

Fleming, David A., ed., *The Fire and the Cloud*, quoted on pp. 70, 72, 73, 124, 142, 146, 199.

Jones, Cheslyn, Geoffrey Wainwright & Edward Yarnold, eds., *The Study of Spirituality*, quoted on pp. 125, 179, 180, 184.

Magill, Frank N. & Ian P. McGreal, eds., *Christian Spirituality*, quoted on p. 95.

zum Brunn, Emilie, & Georgette Epiney-Burgard. *Women Mystics in Medieval Europe*, quoted on pp. 96, 97, 98, 100.

Quotations have also been taken from the following works:

Abhishiktananda, *The Further Shore*, quoted in the *Bulletin of the Abhishiktananda Society*, no. 17, January 1996, here quoted on p. 212.

Abhishiktananda, *Hindu-Christian Meeting Point*. Delhi: I.S.P.C.K., 1969, quoted on p. 216.

Hammarskjöld, Dag, *Markings*, trans. by W. H. Auden & Leif Sjöberg. London, Faber & Faber, 1964, quoted on p. 198.

Sutton, Jonathan, *The Religious Philosophy of Vladimir Solovyov. Towards a Reassessment*. London: Macmillan Press, 1988, quoted on pp. 185, 188.

Should any due acknowledgment have been omitted, we would be pleased to learn of this and to include a correction in future editions.

PICTURE CREDITS

Abbey of St Hildegard, Rüdesheim am Rhein: 83, 123

Hodalic Arne, Ljubljana: 17

C Baumer: 210

Beinecke Rare Book & Manuscript Library, Yale University Library, New Haven, CT: 70 (Ms 404), 111-5 (Ms 404)

Bibliothèque Nationale Universitaire, Strasbourg: 107

Bridgeman Art Library, London: front cover, front cover flap, Contents, 7, 11, 16, 25, 27, 34, 38-39, 41, 45, 53, 55, 62, 67, 76, 86-87, 88, 94, 117, 125, 126, 132, 139, 141, 150, 155, 164, 178, 181, 186, 211, 215 (© Peter Davidson), /Giraudon: 43, 47, 51, 69, 75, 77, 99, 134

British Library, London: 21 (Ms Arun 83 f.129r), 33 (Royal Ms 6E vi f.16r), 118 (Ms Arun 83 f.130v), 122

Bodleian Library, Oxford: 66 (Ms Laud Misc 385 f.41v), 72, 120, 121, 171

Jean-Loup Charmet, Paris: 18-19, 58, 71, 101, 136, 144, 147, 194, 195, 202, 205, 208

Corbis/Paul Almasy: 143, /Roger Wood: 174

Mary Evans Picture Library, London: 36, 84, 153, 157, 162

Fotomas, London: 92, 97

Getty Images, London: 149, 160-61

Sonia Halliday Photographs, Weston Turville: 31, 42, 48, 56, 105, 218, /TC Rising: 22

Robert Harding Picture Library, London/David Beatty: 213

Harper & Brothers, New York: 198

Photothèque André Held, Lausanne: 175

House of St. Gregory & St. Macrina, Oxford: 196 (bottom)

London Library, London: 129, 154, 159, 185, 192, 196 (top)

Magnum Photos, London: /Ernst Haas: 206-7, /Richard Kalvar: BC

National Galleries of Scotland, Edinburgh: 191

Popperfoto, Northampton: 140, 145, 197, 203

Premgit: 216

Antonia Reeve, Edinburgh: 223

Scala Istituto Editoriale SpA, Florence: Frontispiece, 12, 13, 14, 23, 28, 50, 61, 79, 80, 89, 91, 102, 131, 170, 173

SCR Photo Library, London: 169, 189

Tate Gallery, London: 158, 167

Thomas Merton Studies Center, Louisville, KY: 200